Unless otherwise indicated, all scripture quotations are taken from the **King James Version** of the Bible.

PREFACE

1st Timothy 4:12 Let no man despise thy youth; but be thou an example of the believers, in word, in conversation, in charity, in spirit, in faith, in purity. **Vs 15** Meditate upon these things; give thyself wholly to them; that thy profiting may appear to all. **Vs 16** Take heed unto thyself, and unto the doctrine; continue in them: for in doing this thou shalt both save thyself, and them that hear thee.

The above text encapsulates the essence of this book. Drawn from several posts I put on social media, precisely Facebook and Twitter, the articles here were posted over a few years with the aim of encouraging, correcting, and giving guidance to the young minister. I am young too though, but maybe in some cases an older young minister (smiles).

Many young ministers are in need of words that will achieve such. One could be quick to tag many as strange fire, deride the inherent zeal or even sound condescending if not careful, at the youthfulness of many, this cannot serve the gospel if so treated. We need fire, youthfulness and vigour, where wild, just proper guidance but not to douse or destroy.

As you undertake the journey of this compilation, I pray your eyes open to see the glory of Jesus and behold your service for Him and in Him alone.

Take your pen and writing materials. Let us view the heart of Christ to the Young minister!

I call you blessed

Chris Segun Onayinka

Saints Community Church

LESSONS FROM DAVID

CHAPTER ONE

The Epistles teach us to learn from the examples written beforehand.

> **Romans 15:4** For whatsoever things were written aforetime were written for our learning, that we through patience and comfort of the Scriptures might have hope.

We can learn attitudes from the saints of old.

The anointing of David by Samuel must have caught many by surprise. Even the prophet assumed wrongly and his presumption bit the dust.

> **1st Samuel 16:6** And it came to pass, when they were come, that he looked on Eliab, and said, Surely the Lord's anointed is before him.

He probably saw the certificates of Eliab, his looks, his title etc.

> **1st Samuel 16:7** But the Lord said unto Samuel, Look not on his countenance, or on the height of his stature; because I have refused him: for the Lord

seeth not as man seeth; for man looketh on the outward appearance, but the Lord looketh on the heart.

God does not. He looks at the heart. One striking statement was "I have refused him." In the Hebrew language, it sounds like "he failed me"; "failed a test."

Thus, Samuel moved on to the other kids. None was accepted. It is noteworthy only Eliab got specific comments.

It was implied that he should have been the natural choice via natural qualification and age. But not so always.

1st Samuel 16:11 And Samuel said unto Jesse, Are here all thy children? And he said, There remaineth yet the youngest, and, behold, he keepeth the sheep. And Samuel said unto Jesse, Send and fetch him: for we will not sit down till he come hither. **Vs 12** And he sent, and brought him in. Now he was ruddy, and withal of a beautiful countenance, and goodly to look to. And the Lord said, Arise, anoint him: for this is he.

Now, notice the very delicate detail here. He (David)

was not present based on his Dad's reckoning.

But where was he? Keeping the sheep!

Whose sheep? Or what manner of sheep?

Observe, he was anointed and everyone moved on (That will become vital soon).

Much later, the Goliath scenario provides details.

> **1st Samuel 17:17** And Jesse said unto David his son, Take now for thy brethren an ephah of this parched corn, and these ten loaves, and run to the camp to thy brethren; **Vs 18** And carry these ten cheeses unto the captain of their thousand, and look how thy brethren fare, and take their pledge.

His dad even after the anointing sent him on an errand; a menial one. Some latter-day believer would have rejected it, not after the great anointing.

How can a God's general like me take food to my subjects?

Even the apostles served bread and fish (ushering) after healing the sick **(John 6:10-13)**!

That said, Yet he (David) went faithfully.

"Great men are revealed in little things, little men in great things."

The catch in this narrative will soon appear.

> **1st Samuel 17:28** And Eliab his eldest brother heard when he spake unto the men; and Eliab's anger was kindled against David, and he said, Why camest thou down hither? and with whom hast thou left those few sheep in the wilderness? I know thy pride, and the naughtiness of thine heart; for thou art come down that thou mightest see the battle.

Eliab accused him of pride (smarting from the rejection I guess).

Then the issue, "with whom did you leave those **FEW SHEEP**?"

Remember, this sheep belonged to their dad.

Eliab was a stupid man. He spoke in low terms of His patrimony; his Dad's work; sheep.

Like Eliab, we have called God's work "mushroom" as if we are referring to commercial outfits.

David's work was not major. His Bible study group was not much; his Church was small. David however treated the "few sheep" with much dignity, respect and devotion.

1st Samuel 17:20 And David rose up early in the morning, and left the sheep with a keeper, and took, and went, as Jesse had commanded him; ....

If we did not know why Eliab was rejected, now we see.

Also, much later we see why David defeated Goliath.

In his discourse with Saul the (outgoing or 'outgone king) came much more sophisticated detail.

Saul doubted David's capabilities based on his natural appraisal.

David however, had rich experiences which was hitherto insignificant but had now become his asset.

1st Samuel 17:32 And David said to Saul, Let no man's heart fail because of him; thy servant will go and fight with this Philistine. **Vs 34** And David said unto Saul, Thy servant kept his father's sheep, and there came a lion, and a bear, and took a lamb out of the flock: **Vs 35** And I went out after him, and smote him, and delivered it out of his mouth: and when he arose against me, I caught him by his beard, and smote him, and slew him.

He kept the "few sheep" well. Not his own sheep; not his

own ministry. He took on the lion and the bear. No sheep was lost.

He defended the "Insignificant" with his life!

He learnt to fight his battles from insignificant numbers. He learnt pastoring, by discipling two folks. He was not eager for the cheap Facebook/social media crowds gotten via easy friend's acceptance and "likes".

He took his briefs dutifully.

If he had run from the lion and the bear in the Teens Church, or was lazy to pray as a house fellowship leader, or ran away for secular duties as a cell leader, he would never have faced Goliath nor become king!

Let us see another takeaway.

Saul was not fully convinced.

Since this guy was not on TV and had not been to the USA for Bible school, how could he be equipped for this? He must arm him or have a reasonable explanation when his corpse is sent home by Goliath.

Was it a teddy bear or lion king? Saul must have mused, I guess.

Thus, Saul offered his armour.

1st Samuel 17:38 And Saul armed David with his armour, and he put an helmet of brass upon his head; also he armed him with a coat of mail.

You cannot borrow experience, you must have yours. Even if you talk like Reverend so and so, this kind goeth not by copying diction or hairdo or iPad.

David tried it...

1st Samuel 17:39 And David girded his sword upon his armour, and he assayed to go; for he had not proved it. And David said unto Saul, I cannot go with these; for I have not proved them. And David put them off him.

- I cannot go in this!
- I have not proved it!

The maniacal tyranny of learning tips of Church growth from some conferences falls flat here.

During real battles, none of that razzmatazz will work.

Only a spiritual armour birthed and manufactured in your daily experience with God will work. Not backdrops, montage, suits, music, klieg lights etc.

Real armour will be your experience in The Lord.

Your true prayer life, study, meditation (not Facebook copy and paste or read and repackage)

He (David) had a rich experience to rely upon… from **"few sheep"**

Now, I am growing in learning to minister God's word and Spirit over His house. I am still growing.

My deepest experiences are from the insignificant. The years that I taught one to three people for a very long time.

Today, such folks might be wondering how this is.

I once taught **2½** (two and a half) members. One was more of an inconsistent member. But I ensured I did at least four times a week, **3** to **4 hours** daily, with daily fasting.

I personally undertook an all-night prayer every other day… over these "few sheep."

Many of those I learn from and of, have much more deeper experience.

You have to be faithful!

<u>For example:</u>

You cannot ignore your "few sheep" for a ready-made social media crowd.

Minister to them too!

Please do not get me wrong, however the question is: who did God (either via your pastor, leader or otherwise) commit to your trust?

> **Acts 20:28** Take heed therefore unto yourselves, and to all the flock, over the which the Holy Ghost hath made you overseers, to feed the Church of God, which he hath purchased with his own blood.

Whether **two, three, four, ten, or thirty** etc. face your work faithfully.

Fight "their lions and bears!" Pray, fast, do vigils, study etc.

Faithfulness is currency in ministry and service.

In 1993, whilst watching a R.W. Schambach video clip, I sensed The Lord tell me concerning men He used and uses:

"Follow their Labour, toils, faithfulness and not the

results"

I have taken this seriously.

I beseech you fellow labourers; it is time to be faithful with the "few sheep."

> **1st Corinthians 4:2** Moreover it is required in stewards, that a man be found faithful.

So, do it well. Even the menial work like washing Church toilets, cleaning the chairs etc.

I remember in 1994 after I had held a healing meeting with God's power, healing the sick, blind, deaf etc. I attended Youth Foundation Camp Ibadan, and was asked to clean toilets.

Me? Greatest man of God?

Uncle (Pastor) Sola Oladele, the overseer of the ministry rebuked us (me and my co God's generals):

"You mean your anointing will be destroyed by cleaning this toilet?"

I do not know how my friends took it, but I adjusted and

made amends.

To this day, during any of our special programs and even Church services, I get there early to help out. Even as the Pastor with several hundreds of Church workers.

If you want to teach, and last teaching, be faithful.

> **2nd Timothy 2:2** And the things that thou hast heard of me among many witnesses, the same commit thou to faithful men, who shall be able to teach others also.

"Faithful men will always be able, but able men are not always faithful.

Thanks, "uncle" for teaching me this before I started pastoring. I have killed some bears and lions by listening to these details.

Let us therefore be steadfast and faithful.

CHAPTER TWO

One of the critical points in leadership is how you handle your own errors.

You will make mistakes and experience moments of indiscretion.

This can be a lesson for you and others or otherwise.

Scriptures teach us to learn of and from these.

1ˢᵗ Corinthians 10:11 Now all these things happened unto them for ensamples: and they are written for our admonition, upon whom the ends of the world are come. **Vs 12** Wherefore let him that thinketh he standeth take heed lest he fall. **Vs 13** There hath no temptation taken you but such as is common to man: but God is faithful, who will not suffer you to be tempted above that ye are able; but will with the temptation also make a way to escape, that ye may be able to bear it.

Sin remains sin under the two dispensations. Never mind some exuberance of some drunk "grace folks."

David was a man after God's heart.

Hitherto, we learnt of his faithfulness. He learnt to keep "few sheep" and thus could keep God's sheep - Israel.

This does not immune him from temptation and errors.

Let us see a typical one.

> **2nd Samuel 11:2** And it came to pass in an eveningtide, that David arose from off his bed, and walked upon the roof of the king's house: and from the roof he saw a woman washing herself; and the woman was very beautiful to look upon.

Most indiscretions occur during our idle moments, relaxing, surfing the internet; from what we see and read etc.

When you are careless with your eyes and ears, you court sin.

He (David) followed up with a series of actions.

Let us skip these motions, our lessons are weightier and more important than his motions here.

Enter the Prophet Nathan:

> **2nd Samuel 12:7** And Nathan said to David, Thou art the man. Thus saith the Lord God of Israel, I anointed thee king over Israel, and I delivered thee out of the hand of Saul;

He (Nathan) judged him.

Now, a similar incident had happened to his predecessor, it will be of good note to draw some comparisons.

> **1st Samuel 15:13** And Samuel came to Saul: and Saul said unto him, Blessed be thou of the Lord: I have performed the commandment of the Lord. **Vs 14** And Samuel said, What meaneth then this bleating of the sheep in mine ears, and the lowing of the oxen which I hear? **Vs 15** And Saul said, They have brought them from the Amalekites: for the people spared the best of the sheep and of the oxen, to sacrifice unto the Lord thy God; and the rest we have utterly destroyed.

Saul lied. He did what is today called "packaging."

His media team worked a good show, to rebrand; repackage the act.

There is yet more!

> **1ˢᵗ Samuel 15:19** Wherefore then didst thou not obey the voice of the Lord, but didst fly upon the spoil, and didst evil in the sight of the Lord?

God does not do rebranding. Even after the Prophet (Samuel) pointed it out to him, he kept trying to rebrand and repackage it.

Quick check - whilst Samuel ordained (anointed) Saul, Nathan didn't David. So, really Saul should have been in greater deference than David, but not so for haughty personalities.

As soon as they are on air, popular, have seen miracles and crowds, they despise everybody who made their journey so.

Recall:

In **1ˢᵗ Samuel 10**, Saul literally hung on to Samuel's

every word.

1st Samuel 10:1 Then Samuel took a vial of oil, and poured *it* upon his head, and kissed him, and said, *Is it* not because the LORD hath anointed thee *to be* captain over his inheritance? **Vs 2** When thou art departed from me to day, then thou shalt find two men by Rachel's sepulchre in the border of Benjamin at Zelzah; and they will say unto thee, The asses which thou wentest to seek are found: and, lo, thy father hath left the care of the asses, and sorroweth for you, saying, What shall I do for my son? **Vs 3** Then shalt thou go on forward from thence, and thou shalt come to the plain of Tabor, and there shall meet thee three men going up to God to Bethel, one carrying three kids, and another carrying three loaves of bread, and another carrying a bottle of wine: **Vs 4** And they will salute thee, and give thee two *loaves* of bread; which thou shalt receive of their hands. **Vs 5** After that thou shalt come to the hill of God, where *is* the garrison of the Philistines: and it shall come to pass, when thou art come thither to the city, that thou shalt meet a company of prophets coming down from the high place with a psaltery, and a tabret, and a pipe, and a harp, before them; and they shall prophesy: **Vs 6** And the Spirit of the LORD will come upon thee, and thou shalt prophesy with them, and shalt be turned into another man. **Vs 7** And let it be, when these signs are come unto thee, *that* thou do as occasion serve thee; for God *is* with thee. **Vs 8** And thou shalt go down before me to Gilgal; and, behold, I will come down unto thee, to offer burnt offerings, *and* to sacrifice sacrifices of peace offerings: seven days shalt thou tarry, till I come to thee, and shew thee what thou shalt do. **Vs 9** And it was *so,* that when he had turned his back to go from Samuel, God gave him another heart: and all those signs came to pass that day. **Vs 10** And when they came thither to the hill, behold, a company of prophets met him; and the Spirit of God came upon him, and he prophesied among them. **Vs 11** And it came to pass, when all that knew him beforetime saw that, behold, he prophesied among the prophets, then the people said one to another, What *is* this *that* is come unto the son of Kish? *Is* Saul also among the prophets?

Many waters have passed under the bridge, he is now a God's general, an apostle, he now has **5,000** Facebook friends and counting, he is also on YouTube, TBN etc.

Who is Samuel? God merely used him, he could have used another.

That is how we sound when we have become too big in our own eyes.

Let us revisit the texts again.

Two more takeaways.

1st Samuel 15:24 And Saul said unto Samuel, I have sinned: for I have transgressed the commandment of the Lord, and thy words: because I feared the people, and obeyed their voice. **Vs 25** Now therefore, I pray thee, pardon my sin, and turn again with me, that I may worship the Lord. **Vs 26** And Samuel said unto Saul, I will not return with thee: for thou hast rejected the word of the Lord, and the Lord hath rejected thee from being king over Israel.

He (Saul) succumbs eventually, but not in sincerity. He only did because he could see that Samuel had greater insight into the facts.

As said in **verse 22** ...To obey is better than speaking in tongues.

Now, let us examine David.

2nd Samuel 12:13 And David said unto Nathan, I have sinned against the Lord.

That was all he said!

No rebranding, no Press Release, no trying to quickly hold a program to cover up.

Many times, saying **NOTHING** is wiser and sincerer. David saw through this.

Now see the more critical detail.

> **2nd Samuel 12:16** David therefore besought God for the child; and David fasted, and went in, and lay all night upon the earth. **Vs 17** And the elders of his house arose, and went to him, to raise him up from the earth: but he would not, neither did he eat bread with them.

David sought God!

All his ministry team members were not oblivious of his error. His error did not make him less in their sights.

God does this for us.

I hear some preachers boast around like "I do not make mistakes; I have always been walking perfectly in life and ministry."

These are mere Hollywood stunts!

When the cookie crumbles as always, they now run to the media to cover up. You are entitled to God's and our forgiveness, no need to act superficial.

Now, let us read what Saul said:

> **1st Samuel 15:30** Then he said, I have sinned: yet honour me now, I pray thee, before the elders of my

people, and before Israel, and turn again with me, that I may worship the Lord thy God.

What!

- Okay, I agree that I am rejected but let us appear together on the pulpit.
- Let us prophesy together.
- Let men still see me as "anointed."

When the power is off the domestic fans, we now try to get the air to artificially make it work.

Several younger ministers are repeating this error so early. Their ministries rely on media branding, false miracles, testimonies etc.

- Let us just make it appear like it is working!

Rather than seek God, we seek men's attention and approval.

Stupidity!

One day, the chickens will come home to roost.

Craving for limelight has become the pastime of many younger folks, learning the errors of the older ones but not from it.

David was a sincere man! Paul teaches the importance of sincerity in ministry.

> **2nd Corinthians 4:2** But have renounced the hidden things of dishonesty, not walking in craftiness, nor handling the word of God deceitfully; but by manifestation of the truth commending ourselves to every man's conscience in the sight of God.

No dishonesty, half-truths, deceit.

Handle the ministry in truth. It is more appalling that some like sycophants; those who help you with these lies.

Notice:

Paul used the word "we". Ensure you do not build a team of liars; co-liars.

A young ministry must be careful with accolades. I learnt this early enough.

Kenneth E. Hagin would say; "be dead to the praises of men"

David Yonggi Cho reiterated this; "the praises of men are like chewing gum, chew but never swallow"

When we court praises, and rely on the media and

people's applause, we often forget God and the men He uses for us, hence when we go wrong, for us "PR" is more important.

Earlier on, David experienced this temptation.

> **1ˢᵗ Samuel 18:6** And it came to pass as they came, when David was returned from the slaughter of the Philistine, that the women came out of all cities of Israel, singing and dancing, to meet king Saul, with tabrets, with joy, and with instruments of musick. **Vs 7** And the women answered one another as they played, and said, Saul hath slain his thousands, and David his ten thousands.

Do not mind them, David killed Goliath, not thousands.

That is people for you, they will exaggerate your results.

Do not take the poisoned chalice, it is a bait. Remain your sincere self, maintain your innocence and simplicity.

Do not forget you are just a man!

Paul went through the same

> **Acts 14:11** And when the people saw what Paul had

done, they lifted up their voices, saying in the speech of Lycaonia, The gods are come down to us in the likeness of men.

Imagine, a miracle made possible by God's power only.

Yet many will label you "Apostle of the last days," "Paul of our time," "The messenger of the covenant" etc.

Paul responded quickly.

> **Acts 14:15** And saying, Sirs, why do ye these things? We also are men of like **passions** with you, and preach unto you.

The term "passions" means desires, weakness etc.

Stop the nonsense before it stops you. Admit you are human, admit you can be wrong and when you are wrong.

> **1st Timothy 1:19** Holding faith, and a good conscience; which some having put away concerning faith have made shipwreck:

Let us take this cue from David, even in Christ Jesus today.

- A good conscience, a heart that responds to

correction and is dead to adulation and men's exaltation.

Let us be simple, contrite and maintain our innocence.

CHAPTER THREE

David was a leader.

The most intriguing is the fact that he led from youth. Like most of us, he was vulnerable to youthful exuberances.

Yet being young is not an escape route to be unwise, you must be responsible in your conduct

> **2nd Timothy 2:22** Flee also youthful lusts: but follow righteousness, faith, charity, peace, with them that call on the Lord out of a pure heart.

Paul admonishes Timothy several times on this point.

You must yet show good conduct; one worthy of emulation

1st Timothy 4:12 Let no man despise thy youth; but be thou an example of the believers, in word, in conversation, in charity, in spirit, in faith, in purity.

You need not act your age, act the Word.

David had certain exemplary traits we can study for our learning

Romans 15:4 For whatsoever things were written aforetime were written for our learning, that we through patience and comfort of the Scriptures might have hope.

We have seen his faithfulness in little things and his sincerity in faults and failures.

David had respect and honour for authority; Spiritual authority.

Saul was a contrasting personality.

Besides coercing Samuel to appear like all was well, he was a brutal person with power, different from the fellow who had related mildly with Saul earlier on.

1st Samuel 9:21 And Saul answered and said, Am not I a Benjamite, of the smallest of the tribes of Israel? and my family the least of all the families of the tribe of Benjamin? wherefore then speakest thou so to me?

He had now started leading, wealth had come, glamour, power and influence. Enough praise singers.

When God told Samuel to anoint David, Samuel became afraid of Saul.

1st Samuel 16:2 And Samuel said, How can I go? if Saul hear it, he will kill me.

He will use his media influence against me, set his ministers after me, he might destroy my ministry, and has the clout, money and influence.

God understood!

Vs 2 ...And the Lord said; Take an heifer with thee, and say, I am come to sacrifice to the Lord.

Imagine, God's hitherto servant, now lord over all.

1st Peter 5:3 Neither as being lords over God's heritage, but being ensamples to the flock.

He had become the proverbial dog that had failed to heed the master's call.

He became more ferocious.

1ˢᵗ Samuel 18:11 And Saul cast the javelin; for he said, I will smite David even to the wall with it. And David avoided out of his presence twice. **Vs 12** And Saul was afraid of David, because the Lord was with him, and was departed from Saul.

He knew God was with David, yet had no regard for that. His ego was king to him.

David contrasted this.

2ⁿᵈ Samuel 12:25 And he sent by the hand of Nathan the prophet; and he called his name Jedidiah, because of the Lord.

He still deferred to Nathan the Prophet.

He treated Saul with more honour and dignity.

1ˢᵗ Samuel 26:11 The Lord forbid that I should stretch forth mine hand against the Lord's anointed: but, I pray thee, take thou now the spear that is at his bolster, and the cruse of water, and let us go.

- He had several chances to take his own pound of flesh or write on Facebook to "finish Saul off."
- He could have helped online blogs republish stuff about Saul.

Yet he refused!

- The Pulpit must not be used to settle personal scores.

Much later, Saul was killed in battle. What a time to gloat in victory over a competitor in ministry.

David, rather chose to honour.

2nd Samuel 1:4 And David said unto him, How went the matter? I pray thee, tell me. And he answered, That the people are fled from the battle, and many of the people also are fallen and dead; and Saul and Jonathan his son are dead also.

The reporter was assuming this was good news; such and such Church has been closed now... Glory to God!

2nd Samuel 1:5 And David said unto the young man that told him, How knowest thou that Saul and Jonathan his son be dead?

David asked, "how did you know?"

2nd Samuel 1:6 And the young man that told him

said, As I happened by chance upon mount Gilboa, behold, Saul leaned upon his spear; and, lo, the chariots and horsemen followed hard after him.

He had details of the fall of a man of God. He took his time to read up, ask questions, do Facebook chat, Blackberry messaging etc.

Brethren who are telltales must not be allowed near leadership.

Curious fellow!

"If they tell you about others, they will do the same about you to others"

I keep "gist merchants" at arm's length as a matter of principle. I have borne the brunt of their actions!

> **2nd Samuel 1:12** And they mourned, and wept, and fasted until even, for Saul, and for Jonathan his son, and for the people of the Lord, and for the house of Israel; because they were fallen by the sword.

It was not a time to clap and say "I told you so".

Kenneth E. Hagin said "**making your brothers light go dim does not make yours shine brighter**"

A candle loses **NOTHING** if it is used to light another.

> **1st Peter 4:8** And above all things have fervent charity (love) among yourselves: for charity shall cover the multitude of sins.

We must honour those who hurt us too.

Honour those who fail

> **Romans 14:4** Who art thou that judgest another man's servant? to his own master he standeth or falleth. Yea, he shall be holden up: for God is able to make him stand.

Respect them still. Love them.

> **1st Peter 3:8** Finally, be ye all of one mind, having compassion one of another, love as brethren, be pitiful, be courteous:

David gave a decree in all the Land

> **2nd Samuel 1:20** Tell it not in Gath, publish it not in the streets of Askelon; lest the daughters of the

Philistines rejoice, lest the daughters of the uncircumcised triumph.

Note: Two key takeaways:

- We must not rejoice over evil or woe befalling another, we must mourn.

- More so, telling it on social media (Gath) and making it a gist (Askelon) will bring shame to us as well.

I "delete" dishonouring folks from leadership. Till they reform from their stupidity of thinking; since everyone is saying it so should I, forgetting that as an aspiring leader you must act differently.

David was a man of Honour!

Aaron and Miriam were that foolish too.

Numbers 12:1 And Miriam and Aaron spake against Moses because of the Ethiopian woman whom he had married: for he had married an Ethiopian woman... **Vs 9** And the anger of the Lord was kindled against them; and he departed.

It did not matter if social media folks did a Q&A session

on Moses' action, you are a leader and must act differently.

Notice: It took Moses intervention for her to get healed.

In essence, learn honour and respect for authority.

I once spoke with a preacher almost 18 years ago. We were on campus together.

From the obscenities he used against ministers, I guessed he might not be planning to stay long in this work.

I planned to, so even though he was making sense in his sight, I did not contribute.

"What you disrespect, you do not attain"

I must have guessed right, as he has been out of ministry well over 12 years now.

Watch what you spew on social media, private gist etc. Learn from David. Learn from the Scriptures.

With all the nine gifts blazing through you and all the ministry gifts deposited in you, please add honour, as many have trodden this path before and are nowhere to be found.

Hence, stay humble, stay respectful and stay innocent.

CHAPTER FOUR

David served The Lord.

Acts 13:36 For David, after he had served his own generation by the will of God.

He was one of the most quoted characters of the Old Testament, his prophecies were arguably the most quoted, the three longest sermons of the book of Acts had his words in dominance.

1ˢᵗ Corinthians 10:11 Now all these things happened unto them for ensamples: and they are written for our admonition, upon whom the ends of the world are come.

There are examples in David to see and be admonished with.

Romans 15:4 For whatsoever things were written aforetime were written for our learning, that we through patience and comfort of the Scriptures might have hope.

Things to learn from David

One vital truth about his leadership was his commitment to fellowship, devotion and communion.

Psalm 23:6 ...I will dwell in the house of the Lord for ever.

This under the Old Testament referred to devotion.

Despite being the King, despite his busy schedules, teaching and preaching engagements, he found time for communion

Psalms 63:1 O God, thou art my God; early will I seek thee: my soul thirsteth for thee, my flesh longeth for thee.

He had morning devotion frequently.

- Studied and prayed.

Many would have forgotten this tradition as soon as fame, name and gold came.

Since most of their prayer was for things, now that they have things, what's the use anymore, but not David.

Psalms 57:8 Awake up, my glory; awake, psaltery and harp: I myself will awake early.

He was not too busy "serving God" to seek Him.

We hardly know that we need to be more dedicated in leadership to our devotions, communion, than we did before leadership.

Paul had this to say after 30 years of ministry

Philippians 3:10 That I may know him, and the power of his resurrection, and the fellowship of his sufferings, being made conformable unto his death;

After planting apostolic Churches in nations, he was still learning.

Now, let us contrast with David's successor, His son Solomon.

2ⁿᵈ Chronicles 1:10 Give me now wisdom and knowledge, that I may go out and come in before this people: for who can judge this thy people, that is so great?

Solomon started with a right heart.

His request was very unique, such that God commended him

2ⁿᵈ Chronicles 1:11 And God said to Solomon, Because this was in thine heart, and thou hast not asked riches, wealth, or honour, nor the life of thine enemies, neither yet hast asked long life; but hast asked wisdom and knowledge for thyself, that thou mayest judge my people, over whom I have made thee king: **Vs 12** Wisdom and knowledge is granted unto thee; and I will give thee riches, and wealth, and honour, such as none of the kings have had that have been before thee, neither shall there any after thee have the like.

It is noteworthy, how God sees asking for things. Read these verses slowly and see why selfish prayers are never pro-ministry.

That said, most of us start this way - innocent and sincere, but watch this narrative.

> **2nd Chronicles 9:23** And all the kings of the earth sought the presence of Solomon, to hear his wisdom, that God had put in his heart.

He became great and very well-known for revelation knowledge.

He was known for depths in God's word.

His YouTube channel was the most viewed around the world.

His TV program was the most watched.

As usual, he was courted from far and wide

> **2nd Chronicles 9:1** And when the queen of Sheba heard of the fame of Solomon, she came to prove Solomon with hard questions at Jerusalem, with a very great company, and camels that bare spices, and gold in abundance, and precious stones: and when she was come to Solomon, she communed with him of all that was in her heart. **Vs 2** And

Solomon told her all her questions: and there was nothing hid from Solomon which he told her not. **Vs 3** And when the queen of Sheba had seen the wisdom of Solomon, and the house that he had built,

Very astute and very famous. This usually attracts wealth, riches and honour.

All these are God's blessings and Solomon seemed "over blessed."

Now, here goes the issue, the same blessings can be our albatross.

Recall:

- He had built a temple before now (this detail shall become vital very soon).

- The temple was the place for worship, prayers and sacrifice.

He made this apparent in the dedication of that temple.

2nd Chronicles 6:20 That thine eyes may be open upon this house day and night, upon the place whereof thou hast said that thou wouldest put thy name there; to hearken unto the prayer which thy servant prayeth toward this place. **Vs 21** Hearken therefore unto the supplications of thy servant, and of thy people Israel, which they shall make toward this place: hear thou from thy dwelling place, even from heaven; and when thou hearest, forgive.

Jesus reiterated this as well.

Mark 11:17 And he taught, saying unto them, Is it not written, My house shall be called of all nations the house of prayer?

Not only for the Jew.

1ˢᵗ Kings 8:41 Moreover concerning a stranger, that is not of thy people Israel, but cometh out of a far country for thy name's sake; **Vs 42** (For they shall hear of thy great name, and of thy strong hand, and of thy stretched out arm;) when he shall come and pray toward this house;

Even the stranger was to come there to seek God.

Now, here are the intricate issues.

- Solomon never returned there again. He

abandoned that aspect of devotion and fellowship.

- Moreso, rather than the stranger coming to seek God in His house, they came to seek Solomon!

What irony!

We start out showing men Jesus and get distracted by the attraction of fame and fortune and suddenly men are seeking us.

2nd Corinthians 4:5 For we preach not ourselves, but Christ Jesus the Lord; and ourselves your servants for Jesus' sake.

It is now about our testimonies, our exploits, our acquisitions. Men must be like us.

We stop seeking Him, hence those following us foolishly too start seeking us.

In a vision I had in 1995, God showed me His plan for the local Church and every ministry; to have ALL built on the person of His Son; Jesus. The appearance is so mind numbing, it cautions me every now and then.

This has nothing to do with whether you call your ministry or Church, "Jesus only" ministry/Christian center, it is about what you teach, preach, and emphasize!

Solomon became the focus!

The book of Ecclesiastes is his overview of life after repentance.

His summed all "things" as vanity.

Now let us review the symptoms.

- It might appear insignificant initially, a day without prayer turns to a week without devotion, yet you are preaching, teaching even with signs and wonders, just like Solomon, the crowds keep coming and the money too.

Solomon found it comfortable with either non-believers or "carnality."

He had no wars to fight, he had enough "networking" with the godless not to have squabbles with their beliefs.

They spoke in his Church and had an audience in his programmes.

He was no longer strong about discernment.

"We cannot run away from the world", he might have said, but he never visited the temple.

This was unlike his Dad.

> **Psalms 84:10** For a day in thy courts is better than a thousand. I had rather be a doorkeeper in the house of my God, than to dwell in the tents of wickedness.

His Dad was not comfortable with such. He did not emulate his Dad.

> **1ˢᵗ Kings 11:1** But king Solomon loved many strange women, together with the daughter of Pharaoh, women of the Moabites, Ammonites, Edomites, Zidonians, and Hittites;

Since his fellowship with God was weak yet his fellowship with others was waxing strong, strange appetites emerged

> **1ˢᵗ Kings 11:2** Of the nations concerning which the

Lord said unto the children of Israel, Ye shall not go in to them, neither shall they come in unto you: for surely they will turn away your heart after their gods: Solomon clave unto these in love.

Solomon interpreted Scriptures his own way.

"This is the dispensation of grace", he must have said. To the pure, all things are pure!

He never heeded prophecies and warnings. There was no man of God / prophet to talk to him, whom he listened to. This was very much unlike his Dad.

More to come.

> **1st Kings 11:4** For it came to pass, when Solomon was old, that his wives turned away his heart after other gods: and his heart was not perfect with the Lord his God, as was the heart of David his father… **Vs 8** And likewise did he for all his strange wives, which burnt incense and sacrificed unto their gods.

"You cannot rise above the influences you keep around you"

Solomon became worldly. His attention was no longer

The Lord.

No matter how "anointed" you are, the wrong company will destroy you.

I watch the company I keep.

> **1st Corinthians 15:33** Be not deceived: evil communications corrupt good manners.

Do not be deceived!

David had men in his life that could easily discern and judge him.

Solomon had nobody! Except corporate gems, politicians and even some preachers just like him carried away by fame.

He had to follow idols.

The Hebrew and Greek meanings for idolatry imply turning things into objects of adoration.

It need not be "Sango" or "Ogun" (Yoruba deities), just anything that takes your attention off service.

It can be family, friends, things and even Church

members.

Jesus gave us a hint.

> **Matthew 10:37** He that loveth father or mother more than me is not worthy of me: and he that loveth son or daughter more than me is not worthy of me.

More than your quiet time, fasting, study etc., do you create time to listen to God's word or all you hear is yourself?

Leadership should never get into our head.

Good enough, Solomon amended his ways. However, we must not go back to those tracks.

Paul said these to Timothy

> **2nd Timothy 2:4** No man that warreth entangleth himself with the affairs of this life; that he may please him who hath chosen him to be a soldier. **Vs 5** And if a man also strive for masteries, yet is he not crowned, except he strive lawfully.

Be careful with the things of this world!

Kenneth E. Hagin said "I am cautious of anything with the spirit of this world"

I recommend his mini-book "5 hindrances to growing in grace." It is a book for "now."

Paul further warned Timothy .

> **1ˢᵗ Timothy 6:5** Perverse disputings of men of corrupt minds, and destitute of the truth, supposing that gain is godliness: from such withdraw thyself… **Vs 7** For we brought nothing into this world, and it is certain we can carry nothing out.

Note: **Verse 7** is exactly what Solomon meant in Ecclesiastes, many despise this till death tolls, and then they learn it the hard way.

Paul says to withdraw from any minister whose focus is on money.

I endeavour to keep this instruction. I will not watch, listen to or read after you when I notice this about you. Just keeping safe!

> **1ˢᵗ Timothy 6:10** For the love of money is the root of all evil: which while some coveted after, they have erred from the faith, and pierced themselves through with many sorrows. **Vs 11** But thou, O man of God, flee these things; and follow after

righteousness, godliness, faith, love, patience, meekness.

You cannot pursue money in ministry and follow God's plan. The two are incompatible.

Jesus says you cannot serve God and Mammon.

Choose what your emphasis will be, Jesus or You. His person, work, office, message or things.

Like David in **Psalm 42.**

> **Vs 1** As the hart panteth after the water brooks, so panteth my soul after thee, O God.

Let Him be the source and sustainer of our walk and work.

- Be careful for fame, gold and strange friends.

Keep your heart free!

Like John admonished

> **1st John 5:21** Little children, keep yourselves from idols. Amen.

LESSONS FROM JOSHUA

CHAPTER ONE

Joshua is a very good example of a young and wise minister. He served Moses very well.

He was called his servant.

> **Exodus 24:13** And Moses rose up, and his minister Joshua: and Moses went up into the mount of God.

Not God's servant but Moses' servant.

> **Numbers 11:28** And Joshua the son of Nun, the servant of Moses, one of his young men, answered and said, my lord Moses, forbid them.

Same here, he (Joshua) called him (Moses) his lord.

Now, observe what resulted from that.

> **Deuteronomy 34:9** And Joshua the son of Nun was full of the spirit of wisdom; for Moses had laid his hands upon him: and the children of Israel hearkened unto him, and did as the Lord commanded Moses.

His ministry was received.

Laying on of hands works more effectively when there is honour.

Same as Paul and Timothy.

> **2nd Timothy 1:6** Wherefore I put thee in remembrance that thou stir up the gift of God, which is in thee by the putting on of my hands.

Timothy served Paul in the gospel.

> **Philippians 2:22** But ye know the proof of him, that, as a son with the father, he hath served with me in the gospel.

That said

<u>Back to Joshua</u>

Observe what God said about him.

> **Joshua 1:3** Every place that the sole of your foot shall tread upon, that have I given unto you, as I said unto Moses... **Vs 5** There shall not any man be able to stand before thee all the days of thy life: as I was with Moses, so I will be with thee: I will not fail thee,

nor forsake thee.

He stood on Moses' shoulders. Same grace and commission. Just like Timothy, neither of them was trying to be a leader or "connect the anointing" as some would today. They simply served!

Notice, there is more.

It is usually said that he had more exploits than Moses did. At least, he got to the "promised land."

A remarkable exploit never seen before or after him also occurred.

> **Joshua 10:13** And the sun stood still, and the moon stayed, until the people had avenged themselves upon their enemies. Is not this written in the book of Jasher? So the sun stood still in the midst of heaven, and hasted not to go down about a whole day. The earth stopped moving! Time stood still! **Vs 14** And there was no day like that before it or after it, that the Lord hearkened unto the voice of a man: for the Lord fought for Israel.

God heeded a man's voice! Joshua, Moses' servant, never forget. He was not as stupid as Miriam and Aaron who lost their relevance after their indiscreet behaviour in

Numbers 12.

He did not use his mouth to "destroy" his ministry. Rather, he learnt wisdom via Moses' experiences.

I will point one out and continue later on others.

Moses sent out spies, Joshua too did. But in Moses' case, they came back with an evil report.

> **Numbers 13:32** And they brought up an evil report of the land which they had searched unto the children of Israel, saying, the land, through which we have gone to search it, is a land that eateth up the inhabitants thereof; and all the people that we saw in it are men of a great stature.

This caused distress and unbelief in the whole land.

> **Numbers 14:2** And all the children of Israel murmured against Moses and against Aaron: and the whole congregation said unto them, Would God that we had died in the land of Egypt! or would God we had died in this wilderness!

Joshua learnt from this and did it differently. He sent

just two men and discreetly so.

> **Joshua 2:1** And Joshua the son of Nun sent out of
> Shittim two men to spy secretly, saying, Go view the
> land, even Jericho. And they went, and came into an
> harlot's house, named Rahab, and lodged there.

They came back with a faith report.

> **Joshua 2:24** And they said unto Joshua, Truly the
> Lord hath delivered into our hands all the land; for
> even all the inhabitants of the country do faint
> because of us.

More significantly is that unlike Moses' case where and
when the Spies addressed the entire congregation...

> **Numbers 13:26** And they went and came to Moses,
> and to Aaron, and to all the congregation of the
> children of Israel, unto the wilderness of Paran, to
> Kadesh; and brought back word unto them, and unto
> all the congregation, and shewed them the fruit of
> the land.

Joshua ensured that they spoke with him first.

> **Joshua 2:24** And they said unto Joshua, Truly the

Lord hath delivered into our hands...

Then he spoke to the congregation himself

> **Joshua 3:5** And Joshua said unto the people, Sanctify yourselves: for tomorrow the Lord will do wonders among you... **Vs 9** And Joshua said unto the children of Israel, come hither, and hear the words of the Lord your God. **Vs 10** And Joshua said, Hereby ye shall know that the living God is among you, and that he will without fail drive out from before you the Canaanites, and the Hittites, and the Hivites, and the Perizzites, and the Girgashites, and the Amorites, and the Jebusites.

He took charge. He addressed them himself. He taught faith.

Ensure no one does this for you. Joshua learnt from Moses' experience not to repeat this.

Do not expose the congregation to just any sort of information. This was Paul's issue at Galatia.

> **Galatians 2:11** But when Peter was come to Antioch, I withstood him to the face, because he was to be blamed.

Notice, this was not Jerusalem but Antioch, where he had authority and was not supervising the Body of Christ!

That said, Joshua must have truly listened to Moses and took heed not to repeat the same thing the same way.

He also never tried to say "you see the anointing upon me is so unique that things Moses did not see, I saw it".

That would have been both dishonest and dishonourable. Moses must have taught him! As all he did, he learnt from Moses (I will explain this later).

It was the grace on Moses working still. You can learn from the experiences of elders in the faith without disparaging their person.

Our times differ and we have the unique advantage of seeing them and learning from and of them.

Hence, a young minister will do well to learn from Joshua and fulfil God's plan for his own life. As an aside, Aaron was never mentioned in **Hebrews 11** as an elder with exploits of faith, not even Miriam, even though they must have had, Joshua was.

CHAPTER TWO

Joshua learnt how to succeed in ministry.

A basic ingredient was recognizing how important it is to take instructions and not to attempt to reinvent the wheel.

As earlier seen, he was Moses' servant in spirit and truth.

Exodus 24:13 And Moses rose up, and his minister Joshua: and Moses went up into the mount of God.

Not an eyeservice "mentee"or associate but a genuine one.

Paul spoke of this concerning Timothy too.

Philippians 2:20 For I have no man likeminded, who will naturally care for your state. **Vs 21** For all seek their own, not the things which are Jesus Christ's.

He was not a fame seeker but an obedient and truthful associate, unlike hypocrites and eyeservice ones.

> **Philippians 2:12** Wherefore, my beloved, as ye have always obeyed, not as in my presence only, but now much more in my absence.

There are many who turn their backs at your instruction the minute they are on their own or you are not around them.

Even elders too.

> **Acts 20:29** For I know this, that after my departing …**Vs 30** Also of your own selves shall men arise, speaking perverse things, to draw away disciples after them.

Timothy was not like this. Joshua definitely too was not. He hung on to Moses' instructions like God's.

Fans are known for liking what you teach (not necessarily practising them). Church members are known oftentimes for believing it, but Sons and true associates go beyond doctrine alone, they follow your instructions!

That's Joshua for you, the same with Timothy.

1st Timothy 4:15 Meditate upon these things; give thyself wholly to them; that thy profiting may appear to all.

This was not meditation on revelation knowledge but rather instructions that Paul gave him. For ministers, this is where our success lies.

Good doctrine but aided by good obedience to instructions.

Let us view Joshua more closely.

Joshua 1:7 Only be thou strong and very courageous, that thou mayest observe to do according to all the law, which Moses my servant commanded thee: turn not from it to the right hand or to the left, that thou mayest prosper whithersoever thou goest.

He must stick to Moses' instructions to succeed. God kept referring him to Moses! He was wise to follow and follow well.

See this also about him.

Joshua 11:15 As the Lord commanded Moses his servant, so did Moses command Joshua, and so did

Joshua; he left nothing undone of all that the Lord commanded Moses.

He left **NOTHING** undone. He did not try to reinvent the wheel; say something new or try to be his own man. He simply stayed on track.

Now, observe the result of this.

> **Joshua 3:7** And the Lord said unto Joshua, This day will I begin to magnify thee in the sight of all Israel, that they may know that, as I was with Moses, so I will be with thee.

God magnifies faithful men!

Ability always comes with faithfulness, sticking to instructions.

Just like Paul also rightly said;

> **2nd Timothy 2:2** And the things that thou hast heard of me among many witnesses, the same commit thou to faithful men, who shall be able to teach others also.

Notice the terms "same", "of me", "faithful men", and "who shall be able". Their being able is after they are faithful and NOT that they were able before they were faithful.

Joshua knew this plain spiritual principle. He followed Moses' instruction manual to the letter.

He had the spirit of wisdom too.

> **Deuteronomy 34:9** And Joshua the son of Nun was full of the spirit of wisdom; for Moses had laid his hands upon him: and the children of Israel hearkened unto him, and did as the Lord commanded Moses.

Yet, he was wise not to sidestep instructions. Same as Timothy.

> **2nd Timothy 1:14** That good thing which was committed unto thee keep by the Holy Ghost which dwelleth in us.

Joshua followed Moses' instructions till his last breath.

> **Joshua 8:35** There was not a word of all that Moses commanded, which Joshua read not before all the congregation of Israel, with the women, and the little ones, and the strangers that were conversant among them.

Not a word!

Observe, He (Joshua) kept referring to Moses.

> **Joshua 11:23** So Joshua took the whole land, according to all that the Lord said unto Moses; and Joshua gave it for an inheritance unto Israel according to their divisions by their tribes. And the land rested from war.

On the distribution of lands to the children of Israel, he did not say "the Spirit of wisdom told me", rather it was according to Moses' instructions

> **Joshua 22:5** But take diligent heed to do the commandment and the law, which Moses the servant of the Lord charged you, to love the Lord your God, and to walk in all his ways, and to keep his commandments, and to cleave unto him, and to serve him with all your heart and with all your soul.

He kept quoting Moses even though he, not Moses, had the privilege of leading the nation into the Promised Land.

Success did not define him, obedience did.

Some would have jettisoned all this as soon as their ministry became prominent, but not Joshua and Timothy.

Joshua 23:6 Be ye therefore very courageous to keep and to do all that is written in the book of the law of Moses, that ye turn not aside therefrom to the right hand or to the left;

This was a few weeks to his departure. He still had a servant's heart. Kept talking of Moses' instructions. No wonder He was such a phenomenon till the very end.

Joshua 4:14 On that day the Lord magnified Joshua in the sight of all Israel; and they feared him, as they feared Moses, all the days of his life.

Thus, it is vital for young ministers to take instructions as critically as they do doctrinal matters. Your life as a preacher depends on taking heed to instructions.

1st Timothy 4:6 If thou put the brethren in remembrance of these things, thou shalt be a good minister of Jesus Christ, nourished up in the words of faith and of good doctrine, whereunto thou hast attained.

When you listen to instructions given to you by your leader, Pastor or spiritual father you are giving yourself the leeway to prosper.

1ˢᵗ Timothy 4:15 …give thyself wholly to them; that thy profiting may appear to all.

Write down things said to you. Think through them. If prophecies, take note and act upon them.

1ˢᵗ Timothy 1:18 This charge I commit unto thee, son Timothy, according to the prophecies which went before on thee, that thou by them mightest war a good warfare;

They are just as vital as knowing who you are in Christ!

1ˢᵗ Timothy 4:14 Neglect not the gift that is in thee, which was given thee by prophecy, with the laying on of the hands of the presbytery.

Since God has always and will always use men, obeying them is obeying God.

Note: I refer to the men God has sent to you.

CHAPTER THREE

Joshua was a very good student.

Every leader must always be a good student.

> **2ⁿᵈ Timothy 3:14** But continue thou in the things which thou hast learned and hast been assured of, knowing of whom thou hast learned them;

A very critical part of such learning is the spirit of faith. This is not about knowing just doctrine but it is found in your attitude.

Earlier on, this distinguished him (Joshua) amongst the crowd.

> **Numbers 14:6** And Joshua the son of Nun, and Caleb the son of Jephunneh, which were of them that searched the land, rent their clothes:

He did not try to flow with popular views.

Numbers 14:24 But my servant Caleb, because he had another spirit with him, and hath followed me fully, him will I bring into the land whereinto he went; and his seed shall possess it...**Vs 30** Doubtless ye shall not come into the land, concerning which I sware to make you dwell therein, save Caleb the son of Jephunneh, and Joshua the son of Nun.

This was the spirit of faith. Moses had the same spirit of faith.

Hebrews 11:27 By faith he forsook Egypt, not fearing the wrath of the king: for he endured, as seeing him who is invisible.

This was not just in his confession, but seen always in the persistent attitude he had towards God's word to see it fulfilled, which can be termed faithfulness. A child of the faith of God; Moses was properly so called.

Hebrews 3:5 And Moses verily was faithful in all his house, as a servant, for a testimony of those things which were to be spoken after;

Joshua was an example of this too. He was amidst a faithless generation.

Deuteronomy 32:20 And he said, I will hide my face from them, I will see what their end shall be: for they are a very froward generation, children in whom is no faith.

They heard faith but refused to have its spirit; that "God's word will come to pass, against all odds attitude!"

Hebrews 4:2 For unto us was the gospel preached, as well as unto them: but the word preached did not profit them, not being mixed with faith in them that heard it.

Hence they were termed an erring generation

Hebrews 3:10 Wherefore I was grieved with that generation, and said, They do alway err in their heart; and they have not known my ways.

Joshua stood out and "caught" the spirit of faith off Moses. He took God's word above all else. Not to be adjusted to present realities.

Let us view his utterances.

Joshua 1:11 Pass through the host, and command

the people, saying, prepare you victuals; for within three days ye shall pass over this Jordan, to go in to possess the land, which the Lord your God giveth you to possess it.

Notice, no "buts" or "ifs". He was a man of faith!

He must have learnt it by watching Moses, hence he repeated the miracles and even more. He knew faith via teaching and experience.

> **Exodus 17:9** And Moses said unto Joshua, choose us out men, and go out, fight with Amalek: tomorrow I will stand on the top of the hill with the rod of God in mine hand. **Vs 10** So Joshua did as Moses had said to him, and fought with Amalek: and Moses, Aaron, and Hur went up to the top of the hill...**Vs 13** And Joshua discomfited Amalek and his people with the edge of the sword.

This is vital in mentoring; the learner must put things to practice.

That is how to have the spirit of faith. This is different from getting saved.

Jesus did the same to his disciples.

Luke 9:1 Then he called his twelve disciples together, and gave them power and authority over all devils, and to cure diseases. **Vs 2** And he sent them to preach the kingdom of God, and to heal the sick.

They experienced real faith. It had its own flip sides, they needed Jesus' interventions.

Matthew 17:16 And I brought him to thy disciples, and they could not cure him... **Vs 19** Then came the disciples to Jesus apart, and said, Why could not we cast him out?

Yet Jesus taught them with rebuke. They must have caught it afterwards, as they seemed to do more with much boldness.

 Joshua too had Moses correct him and show him how things are done.

Numbers 11:28 And Joshua the son of Nun, the servant of Moses, one of his young men, answered and said, My lord Moses, forbid them. **Vs 29** And Moses said unto him, Enviest thou for my sake? would God that all the Lord's people were prophets, and that the Lord would put his spirit upon them! **Vs 30** And Moses gat him into the camp, he and the elders of Israel.

This was faith in action, not just in words. It is critical in this day and age to ensure you are there to see. Stop relying on social media if and when you should be there.

Many things are taught and a good number are caught!

Timothy had a personal experience with Paul.

> **2ⁿᵈ Timothy 2:2** And the things that thou hast heard of me among many witnesses, the same commit thou to faithful men, who shall be able to teach others also.

He walked with him and saw things, not just via letters.

> **Acts 16:4** And as they went through the cities, they delivered them the decrees for to keep, that were ordained of the apostles and elders which were at Jerusalem. **Vs 5** And so were the Churches established in the faith, and increased in number daily.

> He must have caught things in the process. This only happens when we have vital experience via training.

The spirit of faith is caught. We become rugged, faithful and produce results. Joshua will thus be accorded tremendous regard in history.

Hebrews 11:2 For by it the elders obtained a good report.

He learnt, seeing Moses.

Hebrews 11:30 By faith the walls of Jericho fell down, after they were compassed about seven days.

He now knew to use faith on his own! It sure pays to learn and be available to catch the spirit!

SUBSTITUTING BRASS FOR GOLD?

CHAPTER ONE

2nd Chronicles 12:9 So Shishak king of Egypt came up against Jerusalem, and took away the treasures of the house of the Lord, and the treasures of the king's house; he took all: he carried away also the shields of gold which Solomon had made. **Vs 10** Instead of which king Rehoboam made shields of brass, and committed them to the hands of the chief of the guard, that kept the entrance of the king's house.

The background of this account relates with some instances in some local Churches today. Rather than replace the stolen items with the original specifications for the temple (gold), Rehoboam went for convenience (brass).

The Pentecostal / Charismatic needs to press the restart button in many places today.

I recollect why many trooped out in numbers from the mainline Churches referred to as orthodox Churches. By the way, I believe orthodox is as scriptural for the Church as is charismatic. For the apostles taught order and tradition

> **2nd Thessalonians 3:6** Now we command you, brethren, in the name of our Lord Jesus Christ, that ye withdraw yourselves from every brother that walketh disorderly, and not after the tradition which he received of us.

…Not after the "**tradition**" which he received from us.

> **1st Timothy 3:15** But if I tarry long, that thou mayest know how thou oughtest to behave thyself in the house of God, which is the Church of the living God, the pillar and ground of the truth.

How you ought to behave, not as you are led but as you are instructed.

Even with the charismatic gifts:

> **1st Corinthians 14:33** For God is not the author of confusion, but of peace, as in all Churches of the saints. **Vs 40** Let all things be done decently and in order.

The Church of Jesus is both charismatic and orthodox

(traditional / orderly).

That said.

So, we left for reasons we felt were reducing the Church to mere organizations; no fire for evangelism and prayer

Many people left because the Churches did not encourage firebrand evangelism, door-to-door, bus evangelism, etc. Also, the prayer meetings were hardly attended by anyone, maybe an insignificant fraction of the Church and much more the meetings did not have "fire."

No sound teaching of God's word - many felt most Church leaders even though they went through seminaries could hardly explain Scriptures adequately.

They rather would go into very boring stories, discuss politics etc. The messages were not cutting edge and hardly could call for the sinner to repent and be saved. Many left for smaller Bible study groups and did not care even if they met under mango trees and long as they were teaching Scriptures.

The lust for physical structures - many traditional

Churches invested so much on physical structures. Churches were competing on whose cathedral surpassed the other. At the detriment of spiritual edification came large and beautiful physical edifices.

So, many left and were content with attending a fellowship using classrooms, sitting rooms, under the trees, etc.

Emphasis on money - The numbers of collections during a service alarmed us. Different labels for offerings; different seeds; different envelopes; different collections.

The service could drag on for so long because offerings were being collected.

Thus, we left for new "firebrand" Churches or even Bible study groups which took only ONE offering.

Worldliness - In our view, the traditional Churches were submerged in worldly things in. The clergy was enamoured with Titles; **"Rt. Revd. Dr."** so and so, **"Archbishop"**, **"Bishop"**, **"Apostle"** etc.

We left for simpler things; groups led by Bro John, Pastor Jide. As long as the word was taught and the spirit was "caught" and sinners were won in numbers.

Many services then could at times pass for events, secular discussions and secular speakers.

We left for strong Bible teachings, less ceremonies and less-titled leaders. The Church then paid too much respect to business leaders, politicians and men of societal influence. We left for the unknown but for sound theology, power and prayer.

Ceremonies - The Traditional Church had so many activities. Each week had a different program: Father's Day, Mother's Day, Thanksgiving Sundays etc. We felt they did this to only raise money.

The Church had more events than being eventful for the move of God.

We left for more eventful things outside these events. No room for "this day or that day" or extravaganza.

Now, without sounding critical, some charismatic Churches have taken this same baton and exceeded the traditional Churches in glory.

We pursue erecting structures with greater passion than ensuring we are building men.

We have left the pursuit of training believers for prayer and Evangelism/ministry for success motivation, entrepreneurship etc.

Pray tell, is this not the same condition we complained about?

How are our prayer meetings? Even many of them are filled with praying for our needs, fighting enemies and not praying for others.

How are our services? Programs upon programs, events upon events.

For example, we recently and comfortably joined the secular world in celebrating its days; "this day" and "that day".

Nothing wrong in acknowledging fathers and mothers, but why dedicate an entire Church service to cater to this? Which Scripture did we apply?

To spend weekends celebrating women or men or children! These are the very reasons we left the "orthodox " churches.

Need I say more?

Where are the deep Bible studies?

The single largest services in the '80s was the Deeper Life Bible Church's Bible study that was held on

Mondays.

Men poured in from different denominations, no special announcements, no TV promo, just word-of-mouth telling. Even campus fellowships of Obafemi Awolowo University, then University of Ife, University of Ibadan etc. (All in Nigeria)

The main catch was Bible teaching, prayer, the move of the Spirit etc.

How many Bible studies do we still hold in major Pentecostal Churches?

Do we even have specific teaching emphasis anymore? People hardly even come to Church services with Bibles anymore!

How much importance have we placed on the Scriptures?

With the advent of technology, phones and devices like iPads now replace Bibles. Nothing bad really, only that the same device houses movies, office work, emails, music, pictures etc.

Think about that!

We even project Scriptures on screens, in other words discouraging the bringing of Bibles or taking notes in the services.

Much of leadership now go for titles.

Imagine an undergraduate asking to be called "Pastor" or "Reverend" and some folks inserting apostle to their names or "Dr."

Do we have short memories?

What is our project for training Church workers into able ministers and solid teachers of the word?

The amount of time spent on these "worldly" pursuits of programs and projects could have done more for building spiritual men!

Just as in earlier times, Christians cannot explain their faith, in fact they blend easily in the society.

Thus, like the "orthodox Churches" of old, have we not substituted brass for gold? Have we not given away what was precious to us for what we ran from?

What are we assessing ourselves with? Sunday services / special programs or Bible study and prayer meetings? Church buildings or the Church itself?

Very soon, many of us will experience the same trooping out to more spiritually focused congregations. Hence, the need for us to reform, restart or we lose relevance in the spiritual lives of men.

Let us give ourselves some real thinking.

CHAPTER TWO

What are we building?

The word "building/builded" is used several times in both the Old and New Testament texts of Scriptures.

2nd Chronicles 3:1-3 Then Solomon began to build the house of the Lord at Jerusalem in mount Moriah, where the Lord appeared unto David his father, in the place that David had prepared in the threshingfloor of Ornan the Jebusite. **Vs 2** And he began to build in the second day of the second month, in the fourth year of his reign. **Vs 3** Now these are the things wherein Solomon was instructed for the building of the house of God.

The length by cubits after the first measure was threescore cubits, and the breadth twenty cubits. It was made with physical materials, beautiful artifacts, designs done with very skilled architects and professionals.

Moses had built one earlier, and several others like Nehemiah, Haggai, Ezra etc. were all involved in building for The Lord.

Yet God spoke in this wise

Isaiah 66:1 Thus saith the Lord, The heaven is my throne, and the earth is my footstool: where is the house that ye build unto me? And where is the place of my rest?

He said this whilst a subsisting edifice called "His house" was in place.

Jesus made this comment as well.

John 2:19 Jesus answered and said unto them, Destroy this temple, and in three days I will raise it up.

This sounded ridiculous to the hearers, hence their question

John 2:20 Then said the Jews, Forty and six years was this temple in building, and wilt thou rear it up in three days?

But they were spiritually oblivious.

John 2:21 But he spake of the temple of his body. **Vs 22** When therefore he was risen from the dead, his disciples remembered that he had said this unto them; and they believed the Scripture, and the word which Jesus had said.

For His father's house was not a physical edifice, rather

a spiritual structure, in the Spirit.

Much later he enlightened us further

> **John 14:2** In my Father's house are many mansions: if it were not so, I would have told you. I go to prepare a place for you. **Vs 3** And if I go and prepare a place for you, I will come again, and receive you unto myself; that where I am, there ye may be also.

His Father's house was not the temple built by Moses, Solomon or anyone else. Only Jesus builds the house, needing no engineers.

> **Hebrews 3:6** But Christ as a son over his own house; **whose house are we**, if we hold fast the confidence and the rejoicing of the hope firm unto the end.

And we are this house!

Upon His resurrection, the Father will dwell in believers - His house.

> **John 14:23** Jesus answered and said unto him, If a man love me, he will keep my words: and my Father will love him, and we will come unto him, and make our abode with him.

Hence, he never attempted to build a new temple or

structure for His Church. The Apostles taught this clearly in all their letters.

Hear Paul:

> **1st Corinthians 3:16** Know ye not that ye are the temple of God, and that the Spirit of God dwelleth in you?

The house of God refers to people, not physical buildings.

> **Ephesians 2:21** In whom all the building fitly framed together groweth unto an holy temple in the Lord: **Vs 22** In whom ye also are builded together for an habitation of God through the Spirit.

This house is in the Spirit!

Peter reiterated this as well.

> **1st Peter 2:5** Ye also, as lively stones, are built up a spiritual house, an holy priesthood, to offer up spiritual sacrifices, acceptable to God by Jesus Christ.

It is a spiritual house and it is not purchased with money.

When we gather, this is His house and not where we gather.

Matthew 18:20 For where two or three are gathered together in my name, there am I in the midst of them.

Two or three make up this house as a gathering.

Paul in addressing Timothy pointed this out too.

1st Timothy 3:15 But if I tarry long, that thou mayest know how thou oughtest to behave thyself in the house of God, which is the Church of the living God, the pillar and ground of the truth.

This is our gathering. God dwells in us collectively and individually. Hence when we come together with this consciousness, the unsaved will see this. Not in the venue, but in the congregants

1st Corinthians 14:23 If therefore the whole Church be come together into one place, and all speak with tongues, and there come in those that are unlearned, or unbelievers, will they not say that ye are mad? **Vs 24** But if all prophesy, and there come in one that believeth not, or one unlearned, he is convinced of all, he is judged of all: **Vs 25** And thus are the secrets of his heart made manifest; and so falling down on his face he will worship God, and report that God is in you of a truth.

This happens via his/their experience with us. It is noteworthy that the epistles teach on building as well but definitely not physical structures.

> **1ˢᵗ Corinthians 3:9** For we are labourers together with God: ye are God's husbandry, ye are God's building. **Vs 10** According to the grace of God which is given unto me, as a wise masterbuilder, I have laid the foundation, and another buildeth thereon. But let every man take heed how he buildeth thereupon. **Vs 11** For other foundation can no man lay than that is laid, which is Jesus Christ. **Vs 12** Now if any man build upon this foundation gold, silver, precious stones, wood, hay, stubble;

This is the work of ministry gifts highlighted here. It is not erecting physical structures but spiritual edifices, which is done by teaching, preaching and ministering by the Spirit.

> **1ˢᵗ Corinthians 14:4** He that speaketh in an unknown tongue edifieth himself; but he that prophesieth edifieth the Church…**Vs 12** Even so ye, forasmuch as ye are zealous of spiritual gifts, seek that ye may excel to the edifying of the Church…**Vs 26** How is it then, brethren? when ye come together, every one of you hath a psalm, hath a doctrine, hath a tongue, hath a revelation, hath an interpretation.

Let all things be done unto edifying.

The word "edify" was translated from the Greek word **"oikodomeo"**, it implies erecting a structure and equipping it.

It was translated from the same words used for Solomon's building, however this is with different materials and focus.

This is the ministry of the Local Church.

Ephesians 4:12 For the perfecting of the saints, for the work of the ministry, for the edifying of the body of Christ: **Vs 13** Till we all come in the unity of the faith, and of the knowledge of the Son of God, unto a perfect man, unto the measure of the stature of the fulness of Christ: **Vs 14** That we henceforth be no more children, tossed to and fro, and carried about with every wind of doctrine, by the sleight of men, and cunning craftiness, whereby they lie in wait to deceive; **Vs 15** But speaking the truth in love, may grow up into him in all things, which is the head, even Christ: **Vs 16** From whom the whole body fitly joined together and compacted by that which every joint supplieth, according to the effectual working in the measure of every part, maketh increase of the body unto the edifying of itself in love.

This is the building the local Church ought to engage in. Whilst we must seek, search, secure and if necessary purchase places of gathering, it **MUST** never replace the building God looks for and seeks.

Jesus discarded the emphasis on the place to the People

> **John 4:21** Jesus saith unto her, Woman, believe me, the hour cometh, when ye shall neither in this mountain, nor yet at Jerusalem, worship the Father… **Vs 23** But the hour cometh, and now is, when the true worshippers shall worship the Father in spirit and in truth: for the Father seeketh such to worship him…**Vs 24** God is a Spirit: and they that worship him must worship him in spirit and in truth.

Hence, the spiritual edification of believers when we gather.

It is noteworthy that for about 1000 years after the ascension of Jesus, the Church did not own properties or real estate. Yet, it influenced cities and nations.

In fact, the book of Acts and the Epistles mentioned with strong emphasis that the homes of the saints were used for the Church gatherings.

Acts 2:46 And they, continuing daily with one accord in the temple, and breaking bread from house to house, did eat their meat with gladness and singleness of heart,

Acts 20:20 And how I kept back nothing that was profitable unto you, but have shewed you, and have taught you publickly, and from house to house,

Romans 16:5 Likewise greet the Church that is in their house. Salute my wellbeloved Epaenetus, who is the firstfruits of Achaia unto Christ.

Erecting of structures was never mentioned but rather building of believers spiritually.

Let us examine what happened in Ephesus.

Acts 19:9 But when divers were hardened, and believed not, but spake evil of that way before the multitude, he departed from them, and separated the disciples, disputing daily in the school of one Tyrannus...**Vs 20** So mightily grew the word of God and prevailed.

The influence of the message grew with great power.

Today, for modernity's sake, we might need to get

spaces to meet and gather. At times, very large spaces if our congregants are as much.

But we MUST never think this is our focus. Our work is to build men.

If the Church in the Apostles' days were into tens of thousands, yet did not erect structures but had immense influence, the Church of today needs to refocus.

The people or the venue?

 Property or spiritual growth?

Architectural designs or gifts (things) of the Spirit?

How much focus are we placing on our teaching, prayer and gifts of the spirit in operation amongst us?

Are we building saints or cathedrals in place of saints?

Note: You cannot build the Church with engineers. You can only build it with the Word.

It is noteworthy that what we received from Our Lord Jesus and the Apostles is the teaching of the gospel.

That is what will last and outlast buildings and physical structures,

Thus, before we embark on a Church building project which can be necessary, we must ask if we have placed spiritual growth above this. Otherwise, the same fate that befell cathedrals of yore, with massive and enormous heights but today are standing carcasses and caricatures, will yet befall our massive and eye catching structures eventually.

Let us value men above buildings.

Let us build men!

CHAPTER THREE

How not to treat the youths?

Youths are not as restless and excitement-focused as we think. It is an appetite we have created and also feeding.

The mainline denominations back then suffered for not training the youth for ministry.

Paul stated in unequivocal terms the focus of ministry gifts

> **Ephesians 4:11** And he gave some, apostles; and some, prophets; and some, evangelists; and some, pastors and teachers; **Vs 12** For the perfecting of the saints, for the work of the ministry, for the edifying of the body of Christ:

For the work of ministry!

This is the true proof of growth. Thus, the youth must be engrafted into this plan.

David was a young shepherd boy, who became king over a nation.

> **1st Samuel 16:11** And Samuel said unto Jesse, Are

here all thy children? And he said, There remaineth
yet the youngest, and, behold, he keepeth the sheep.
And Samuel said unto Jesse, Send and fetch him: for
we will not sit down till he come hither. **Vs 12** And
he sent, and brought him in. Now he was ruddy, and
withal of a beautiful countenance, and goodly to look
to. And the Lord said, Arise, anoint him: for this is
he. **Vs 13** Then Samuel took the horn of oil, and
anointed him in the midst of his brethren: and the
Spirit of the Lord came upon David from that day
forward. So Samuel rose up, and went to Ramah.

He was a prophet from his teenage years. Same with
many others.

Another example is Jeremiah.

Jeremiah 1:6 Then said I, Ah, Lord God! behold, I
cannot speak: for I am a child. **Vs 7** But the Lord said
unto me, Say not, I am a child: for thou shalt go to all
that I shall send thee, and whatsoever I command
thee thou shalt speak.

Today, both probably would have been secondary
school students. Same as the Lord Jesus.

Luke 2:42 And when he was twelve years old, they
went up to Jerusalem after the custom of the
feast...**Vs 46** And it came to pass, that after three

days they found him in the temple, sitting in the midst of the doctors, both hearing them, and asking them questions...**Vs 47** And all that heard him were astonished at his understanding and answers.

At age twelve, he was not occupied by his local Church with concerts, festivals, dance or talk shows. Rather, He was into deep and intense Bible study.

Another example was Timothy.

> **Acts 16:1** Then came he to Derbe and Lystra: and, behold, a certain disciple was there, named Timotheus, the son of a certain woman, which was a Jewess, and believed; but his father was a Greek: **Vs 2** Which was well reported of by the brethren that were at Lystra and Iconium. **Vs 3** Him would Paul have to go forth with him; and took and circumcised him because of the Jews which were in those quarters: for they knew all that his father was a Greek.

He was a teenager known for ministry effectiveness in his local Church.

The Youth are God's men, not some hyperactive blood, looking for expressions in the flesh.

Paul's instruction to Timothy calls for reflection.

> **1st Timothy 4:12** Let no man despise thy youth; but be thou an example of the believers, in word, in conversation, in charity, in spirit, in faith, in purity. **Vs 13** Till I come, give attendance to reading, to exhortation, to doctrine. **Vs 14** Neglect not the gift that is in thee, which was given thee by prophecy, with the laying on of the hands of the presbytery. **Vs 15** Meditate upon these things; give thyself wholly to them; that thy profiting may appear to all. **Vs 16** Take heed unto thyself, and unto the doctrine; continue in them: for in doing this thou shalt both save thyself, and them that hear thee.

Paul was clear; be an example to **ALL** believers and not just the young; give yourself to doctrine and not to fun Places; the emphasis was on supernatural gifts and not talent.

The Orthodox Church of old gave little focus to giving spiritual training to the young. They allowed many to waste their youthfulness till the "revivalists" came and made adequate use of the youth; prayer meetings, evangelism and Bible study.

It was first termed exuberance till many grew into movements and are overseeing many of the most influential ministries around the world today.

The charismatic Churches are making similar errors.

Whilst not ignoring the youth totally, we are making a worse error by feeding the youth with fun, excitement, romance, talk shows, concerts, success motivation etc.

These are things they can and will get, with far better expertise outside the Church.

I was brought up by the Youth **Foundation Ministry** under Uncle (Pastor) Sola Oladele. I learnt fasting and prayer, personal holiness, evangelism, and ministry there.

I did not need a voice to be called into ministry. All our weekly activities even as secondary school students were filled with either Bible study, ministers' meetings, prayer meetings, group meetings etc.

No room for razzmatazz, they took us on retreats, prayer, fasting and spiritual exercises. It was very easy to obey God.

Thus, we must keep reminding the youth on these basics; the very core of ministry, peradventure they seek to follow the multitudes in our day.

It is a pity, we have done little in this regard. We have kept the youth with non-spiritual things.

Very soon, they will find out they can get the same elsewhere and better.

Let us reform! The youth is the training ground for the move of God.

Campus fellowships, however, are now the breeding grounds for success motivators and romance experts. Sad!

These same places birthed hundreds/thousands of missionaries, apostles, etc. The revival then had nothing to do with materialism but spiritual rejuvenation.

Today, many **"oldies"** are not even ashamed to go there and "inspire" the younger generation with some worldly exploits.

Where are our signs? If we are to have more "Davids", "Timothys", we must change our approach.

Let us get back the old culture. Times can change but God will not and neither will His word nor the needs of man or the old the wily devil.

Let us get back to the trenches.

Dear minister do not give the younger generation less of what you received; full blooded and rigorous spiritual discipline, days of fasting and prayer, exercise of the gifts of the Spirit, deep and intense Bible study etc.

The kind of things that birthed the move of God in the '70s and '80s.

If we continue in this inglorious path for populism, its limits are almost here and we shall be exactly what we ran away from.

Get the youths back to spiritual things!

ON SPIRITUAL MENTORSHIP

Things Paul told Timothy - Understanding ministry mentorship (1)

We have just one major model of ministerial training, mentorship and fathering in the epistles. Paul and Timothy, and also Titus.

It is noteworthy that Timothy was very active in ministry, "a pastor of pastors," yet he was undergoing training.

This piece would let you know if you are being well mentored or mentoring others well too.

Let us see some instructions that Paul gave him

1st Timothy 1:3 As I besought thee to abide still at Ephesus, when I went into Macedonia, that thou mightest charge some that they teach no other doctrine, **Vs 4** Neither give heed to fables and endless genealogies, which minister questions, rather than godly edifying which is in faith: *so do*.

Stop false teaching and its teachers. Do not give room for false teaching either.

1st Timothy 1:18 This charge I commit unto thee, son Timothy, according to the prophecies which went before on thee, that thou by them mightest war a good warfare; **Vs 19** Holding faith, and a good conscience; which some having put away concerning faith have made shipwreck:

- Do not despise supernatural utterances

- "Holding faith…," which refers to the message

- Know that some folks have abandoned ship, they have gone after false doctrines.

The post-text mentioned their names. Hence, Paul delivered them to Satan, which means condemnation.

1st Timothy 2:1 I exhort therefore, that, first of all, supplications, prayers, intercessions, and giving of thanks, be made for all men;

Prayer!

You must pray and be prayerful!

1st Timothy 2:8 I will therefore that men pray everywhere, lifting up holy hands, without wrath and doubting.

Ensure those in Church do too

1st Timothy 3:1 This is a true saying, If a man desire the office of a bishop, he desireth a good work. **Vs 2** A bishop then must be blameless, the husband of one wife, vigilant, sober, of good behaviour, given to hospitality, apt to teach;

Those to be placed in leadership must be sound. Do not just put anyone

1st Timothy 3:8 Likewise must the deacons be grave, not double-tongued, not given to much wine, not greedy of filthy lucre…**Vs 10** And let these also first be proved; then let them use the office of a deacon, being found blameless…**Vs 14** These things write I unto thee, hoping to come unto thee shortly: **Vs 15** But if I tarry long, that thou mayest know how thou oughtest to behave thyself in the house of God, which is the Church of the living God, the pillar and ground of the truth.

There should be order in how you do things, the emphasis here is on choosing leadership

> **1ˢᵗ Timothy 4:6** If thou put the brethren in remembrance of these things, thou shalt be a good minister of Jesus Christ, nourished up in the words of faith and of good doctrine, whereunto thou hast attained. **Vs 7** But refuse profane and old wives' fables, and exercise thyself rather unto godliness.

Ensure you warn the Church about false doctrine, so that you are a good minister. You should shun false doctrine too.

> **1ˢᵗ Timothy 4:11** These things command and teach.

Teach these things with authority.

> **1ˢᵗ Timothy 4:12** Let no man despise thy youth; but be thou an example of the believers, in word, in conversation, in charity, in spirit, in faith, in purity.

No one should look down on you, do not permit it. Rather than get defensive, be exemplary.

> **1ˢᵗ Timothy 4:14** Neglect not the gift that is in thee,

which was given thee by prophecy, with the laying on of the hands of the presbytery. **Vs 15** Meditate upon these things; give thyself wholly to them; that thy profiting may appear to all. **Vs 16** Take heed unto thyself, and unto the doctrine; continue in them: for in doing this thou shalt both save thyself, and them that hear thee.

- Never forget the supernatural gift.
- Meditate upon my instructions
- Be careful about what you teach.
- Save yourself and your audience!

Note: nothing here suggests several things taught in some schools of ministry.

Paul did not teach him; How to grow your ministry, be relevant or covenant secrets of world renowned ministries or mysteries of the fastest growing ministers. For instance; fasting, the media etc.

Nothing in these letters suggests they were implied, rather more of **caution** was taught.

Things Paul told Timothy - Understanding ministry mentorship (2)

As earlier said, the letters Paul wrote to Timothy and Titus are our major benchmarks for mentorship in the epistles.
Timothy was a man under training.

Nothing suggests Paul set him any material or numerical standards.

Nothing! Much of what is training is caution.
This will help you receive mentorship and give the same too.

> **1 Timothy 5:1** Rebuke not an elder, but intreat him as a father; and the younger men as brethren; **Vs 3** Honour widows that are widows indeed. **Vs 11** But the younger widows refuse: for when they have begun to wax wanton against Christ, they will marry;

Know how to treat different classes of people in the Church. Elders, widows (old and young).

No partiality!

> **1 Timothy 5:17** Let the elders that rule well be counted worthy of double honour, especially they who labour in the word and doctrine. **Vs 18** For the Scripture saith, Thou shalt not muzzle the ox that treadeth out the corn. And, The labourer is worthy of his reward.

Ensure teachers are well remunerated.
This is proof of honour for the ministry of the Word

> **1 Timothy 5:19** Against an elder receive not an accusation, but before two or three witnesses. **Vs 20** Them that sin rebuke before all, that others also may fear.

Learn to discipline elders who err before all.
This impliedly deals with public error.
It is for others to learn

> **1 Timothy 5:23** Drink no longer water, but use a little wine for thy stomach's sake and thine often infirmities.

He speaks about his health which is of no direct doctrinal probative value, however he lets us see two critical things.

Firstly, Paul is also concerned about Timothy's natural welfare.
Secondly, it's not "unapostolic" to fall ill, and in this case often.

> **1 Timothy 6:1** Let as many servants as are under the yoke count their own masters worthy of all honour, that the name of God and his doctrine be not blasphemed. **Vs 2** And they that have believing masters, let them not despise them, because they are brethren; but rather do them service, because they are faithful and beloved, partakers of the benefit. These things teach and exhort.

The is a total departure from success motivation.
He instructs him to teach employees to serve well, not to **"fire your boss"**

Also, not to take advantage of their being believers.
All in all, Paul's instructions were on Christian conduct, **not** entrepreneurship secrets.

> **1 Timothy 6:3** If any man teach otherwise, and consent not to wholesome words, even the words of our Lord Jesus Christ, and to the doctrine which is according to godliness;

Now as a post text, any teaching otherwise is not godly.

1 Timothy 6:5 Perverse disputings of men of corrupt minds, and destitute of the truth, supposing that gain is godliness: from such withdraw thyself.

Do not associate with ministers who attach material blessings to serving God. He has very strong adjectives for them,

Company affects us all.

1st Timothy 6:9 But they that will be rich fall into temptation and a snare, and into many foolish and hurtful lusts, which drown men in destruction and perdition. **Vs 10** For the love of money is the root of all evil: which while some coveted after, they have erred from the faith, and pierced themselves through with many sorrows. **Vs 11** But thou, O man of God, flee these things; and follow after righteousness, godliness, faith, love, patience, meekness.

FLEE...

- From your desires
- From those who love money

It will change your doctrine. You will soon start revising your teaching and emphasis.

1st   Timothy   6:14   That   thou   keep   this commandment without spot, unrebukeable, until the appearing of our Lord Jesus Christ:

Be pure in your teaching and the instructions that I gave you.

1st Timothy 6:17 Charge them that are rich in this world, that they be not highminded, nor trust in uncertain riches, but in the living God, who giveth us richly all things to enjoy;

Warn the rich not to build trust on Money.

1st Timothy 6:20 O Timothy, keep that which is committed to thy trust, avoiding profane and vain babblings, and oppositions of science falsely so called:

Again; **"avoid"**, **"keep"**

Note: Once again, we see much of caution and carefulness; Things and people to avoid.

His teaching emphasis is also put in view. No secrets for success for global ministry!

He urged him to ensure he is blameless before Christ's judgment seat. Ultimately!

Things Paul told Timothy - Understanding ministry Mentorship (3)

We have seen so far that mentorship scripturally entails no spiking of ambition as some do today.

They inspire themselves to "reach targets"; 100,000-seater auditoriums, etc.

That is not found in any strand of these letters, written to Timothy (and Titus) which encapsulates ministry mentorship.

Let us examine them again.

> **2ⁿᵈ Timothy 1:6** Wherefore I put thee in remembrance that thou stir up the gift of God, which is in thee by the putting on of my hands. **Vs 7** For God hath not given us the spirit of fear; but of power, and of love, and of a sound mind.

Do not allow timidity hinder the operations of the gift of

God. He reinforces this much.

Mentors do not inspire fear even if they must caution. True mentors provide an environment for your gifts to flourish.

> **2ⁿᵈ Timothy 1:8** Be not thou therefore ashamed of the testimony of our Lord, nor of me his prisoner: but be thou partaker of the afflictions of the gospel according to the power of God;

You must not be ashamed of the message. Much suffering and mockery comes with it. Ensure you stand strong.

> **2ⁿᵈ Timothy 1:1** Hold fast the form of sound words, which thou hast heard of me, in faith and love which is in Christ Jesus. **Vs 14** That good thing which was committed unto thee keep by the Holy Ghost which dwelleth in us. **Vs 15** This thou knowest, that all they which are in Asia be turned away from me; of whom are Phygellus and Hermogenes.

Another buzz for doctrinal purity.

That is what the Holy Ghost gave you, not some vision, dream or weird encounter.

Now, notice a fundamental issue here; the sudden departure of many in Asia. Asia was where Paul's ministry had the greatest influence.

Hence the need to keep Timothy's focus.

Timothy was probably facing this sudden change of followership by many whom he should know. Hence the need to stay strong.

Today, this would have been termed failure, but it is not up to you how people keep the faith, rather, it is up to you how you keep it!

> **2nd Timothy 2:1** Thou therefore, my son, be strong in the grace that is in Christ Jesus.

This flows from the earlier chapter.

The phrase **"Be strong"** here relates with the message. We all need this so very often

> **2nd Timothy 2:2** And the things that thou hast heard of me among many witnesses, the same commit thou to faithful men, who shall be able to teach others also.

Much more, he instructs Him to keep committing the same to loyal men. Loyal to the message, not some shifting fellow.

This is an important aspect of leadership; you must know and recognize faithful men.

The message works better with such folks. This makes sense in the apparent apostasy happening to the Pauline revelation.
This is needed in mentorship.

> **2nd Timothy 2:3** Thou therefore endure **hardness**, as a good soldier of Jesus Christ. **Vs 4** No man that warreth entangleth himself with the affairs of this life; that he may please him who hath chosen him to be a soldier.

Hardness here again relates to the message and not any other.

Too many fairweather people will be seen when hardship is seen; persecution, difficulty, lack of support, etc.

You must endure, not for "success" but to please Christ!

> **2nd Timothy 2:7** Consider what I say; and the Lord give thee understanding in all things. **Vs 8** Remember that Jesus Christ of the seed of David was raised from the dead according to my gospel:

He reminds him of the message in its simple terms.

Many times mentors ensure they give you very brief mission statements of the gospel, summations of all that is taught and believed, so we never lose focus.

> **2nd Timothy 2:14** Of these things put them in remembrance, charging them before the Lord that they strive not about words to no profit, but to the subverting of the hearers **Vs 15 Study** to shew thyself approved unto God, a workman that needeth not to be ashamed, rightly dividing the word of truth. **Vs 16** But shun profane and vain babblings: for they will increase unto more ungodliness.

You must ensure you make the defense of the message very often before the Church.

The term "study" means "be eager; work hard; be diligent"

The man of God easily loses zeal amid difficulties and hardship.

You must be diligent in teaching and be much more precise and strong on what you believe. Again, beware of wrong doctrine, shun them, do not respect them, quote or reference them.

2ⁿᵈ Timothy 2:22 Flee also youthful lusts: but follow righteousness, faith, charity, peace, with them that call on the Lord out of a pure heart.

FLEE! Run from your own desires.

A mentor keeps you focused on self-control

2ⁿᵈ Timothy 2:23 But foolish and unlearned questions avoid, knowing that they do gender strifes. **Vs 24** And the servant of the Lord must not strive; but be gentle unto all men, apt to teach, patient, **Vs 25** In meekness instructing those that oppose themselves; if God peradventure will give them repentance to the acknowledging of the truth;

Avoid stupid discussions; subjects that mean nothing in the gospel. However, endeavour to teach your opponents.
Do not baulk at the chance to let them see the truth of God's word, but do it in meekness and not with an "I know more than you" attitude.

Note: Once again, we see mentoring.

- No quick fixes, gathering of crowds mentioned

- Acquiring assets? Not mentioned.

It appears unlike the earlier letter, the second focuses

more on consistency.

Many of us need mentors. They keep us in the faith; the truth of the gospel.

They help us not to get ahead of ourselves. Not fueling ambitions.

Things Paul told Timothy - Understanding ministry Mentorship (4)

You cannot mentor without deep and rich experience. That is clear here.

You do not become a mentor simply because you have a congregation. It is beyond that.

Paul had a very definite message birthed and well known over a long period of time.

Let us examine a few more things

> **2nd Timothy 3:1** This know also, that in the last days perilous times shall come.

He reminds him of the difficult times; opposition to the

gospel. False doctrine was abounding and this led to many abandoning ship.

Notice: For Timothy to stay still, evokes thoughts of a loyal person.

Strange teachings signify perilous times. Last days never refer to before the rapture as much as the times after Christ's death

During the fulfillment of God's promises in Christ, will come opposition to its truths. You must be prepared. This is what mentors do… **Prepare You!**

> **2nd Timothy 3:14** But continue thou in the things which thou hast learned and hast been assured of, knowing of whom thou hast learned them;

So much preceded and proceeded from this statement. All hinged on this.

You must recognize your teacher, from whom you have learnt and are learning. Not his Facebook friends, associates, friends.

Notice: **"…Of whom"**

This was needed!

Mentors need to do this reminder very often lest we stray, thinking all men are the same to us.

It is succinct however that this was based on faith in Christ alone, as **verse 15-17** showed.

> **2nd Timothy 4:2** Preach the word; be instant in season, out of season; reprove, rebuke, exhort with all longsuffering and doctrine. **Vs 5** But watch thou in all things, endure afflictions, do the work of an evangelist, make full proof of thy ministry.

Yes! Preach the message **ONLY**.

Do not yield to pressures from your members or the society. They will start thinking the message is no more relevant.

Do not take the bait! In season and out of season, say the same things.

No "secret of the quantum leap of Isaac in this recession", Finding your marriage partners etc. If it was not there do not add it.

Mentorship keeps us in check!

From experience, Paul could see that Timothy could buckle under pressure

Mentors keep our focus on Christ. Not the crowd!

2nd Timothy 4:7 I have fought a good fight, I have finished my course, I have kept the faith:

This is the High point of all he said to him…"My" or "the course". The faith!

Not my universities, buildings, TV stations, my trips across the world or miracles

Note: False teachers have numbers, buildings, global reach too.

That was why Asia left Paul!

You do not judge ministry with people's reception. Judge it from the word.

You were sent to reach men but do not let them dictate to you. Be focused!

A mentor stresses the importance of keeping the message. Not keeping attendance, but the message. Not the finance or influence, but the message. That is what will eventually count.

True mentors will save us from ourselves and the crowd

too. Paul expects Timothy to look at ending this way too.

2ⁿᵈ Timothy 4:10 For Demas hath forsaken me, having loved this present world, and is departed unto Thessalonica; Crescens to Galatia, Titus unto Dalmatia. **Vs 11** Only Luke is with me. Take Mark, and bring him with thee: for he is profitable to me for the ministry. **Vs 12** And Tychicus have I sent to Ephesus. **Vs 13** The cloke that I left at Troas with Carpus, when thou comest, bring with thee, and the books, but especially the parchments.

These statements show relationship, trust, Deep association. Mentorship must involve more than mere surface issues.

Paul could mention names, issues, non-doctrinal objects etc. This is very substantial. He counseled him on Mark, he expects him to take his word for it. That is mentorship.

Trust is inbuilt! No manipulation but fondness, intimacy and relationship. This is mentorship!

2ⁿᵈ Timothy 4:14 Alexander the coppersmith did me much evil: The Lord reward him according to his works: **Vs 15** Of whom be thou ware also; for he hath greatly withstood our words.

He warns him of a Person. It is very healthy. If he can write against me, be careful with him.

Truth is, Paul fathered Timothy. Thus, you can not oppose Paul and be Timothy's friend. Else Timothy is a Hypocrite. This is true mentorship.

Some are political about relationships. They are neither here nor there. Not healthy folks. You must be seen as straight and plain. Mentors must disclose those who oppose them, it guides us, else we are deceived.

This opposition is against the message!

> **2nd Timothy 4:19** Salute Prisca and Aquila, and the household of Onesiphorus.

A close note here situates the relationship; he could ask him to do felicitating on his behalf. That's a fabric of this relationship. This is very fundamental.

Note: It is clear therefore that the MOST pivotal part of mentorship is doctrine.

Doctrine includes instructions. Relationships not birthed via teaching cannot be scriptural mentorship.

Again nothing to aspire for but ONLY to stay on course with the message and please Christ despite pressures, demands, desires, popular issues.

Is this how you are being mentored, have been mentored or are mentoring others?

Ask these questions now before it is too late.

Things Paul told Timothy - Understanding ministry mentorship (conclusion)

As earlier explained, Paul and Timothy (with Titus) are our major New Testament father-son; mentorship examples.

Much lies in Paul's letters to them on leadership.

We can summarize them in few words

"Keep, stay, know, flee, preach, avoid, withdraw, pray, be diligent, stir up, neglect not, be bold, be not ashamed, keep yourself pure, keep your doctrine pure, do not want to be rich, do not serve God for money, watch your company, watch your desires, be an example, take heed, do not follow crowds they come and go ...etc."

All towards one purpose...To please Christ, stand before

him having kept the message!

As a final note, it was obvious crowd appeal was NEVER proof of fulfilling ministry. Crowds will come and go.

Paul once had Asia, then lost it again.

But one thing you must NEVER lose, is the **MESSAGE.**

The Father and My Father... (Examining the concept of a Father in the Lord or Spiritual Father)

Matthew 23:9 And call no man your father upon the earth: for one is your Father, which is in heaven.

Someone with the aid of the above text approached me with the aim of finding out if the concept of referring to another believer as your "Father in the Lord" is not an error.

Below are (were) my answers:

A basic rule of Bible study is contextual reading.

It goes thus:

Read the pretext (several verses before the text). It is safest to start where the maker of the statement began or where the statement under study takes its distinction from.

Observe also, that words like "therefore" are conditional, "but" infers an exception or a contrast, "now" many times in old grammatical texts means therefore e.g. **1st John 3:2, Hebrews 11:1** etc.

Read the post text (several verses after the text), this helps understand the destination of the statement else you might end up picking words like;

"Judas went to hang himself..., ...go and do likewise..., ...whatever you need to do..., ...do quickly"

Obviously, this is what reading Scriptures out of context does!

<u>So, back to the text (**Matthew 23:9**)</u>

Previous verses

Matthew 23:2-8 Saying, The scribes and the Pharisees sit in Moses' seat: **Vs 3** All therefore whatsoever they bid you observe, that observe and do; but do not ye after their works: for they say, and do not. **Vs 4** For they bind heavy burdens and grievous to be borne, and lay them on men's shoulders; but they themselves will not move them with one of their fingers. **Vs 5** But all their works they do for to be seen of men: they make broad their phylacteries, and enlarge the borders of their garments, **Vs 6** And love the uppermost rooms at feasts, and the chief seats in the synagogues, **Vs 7** And greetings in the markets, and to be called of men, Rabbi, Rabbi. **Vs 8** But be not ye called Rabbi: for one is your Master, even Christ; and all ye are brethren.

He obviously was referring to the hypocrisy of the Pharisees.

The proceeding verses;

Matthew 23:10 Neither be ye called masters: for one is your Master, even Christ. **Vs 11** But he that is greatest among you shall be your servant. **Vs 12** And whosoever shall exalt himself shall be abased; and he that shall humble himself shall be exalted. **Vs 13** But woe unto you, scribes and Pharisees, hypocrites! for ye shut up the kingdom of heaven against men: for ye neither go in yourselves , neither suffer ye them that are entering to go in. **Vs 14** Woe unto you, scribes and Pharisees, hypocrites! For ye devour widows' houses, and for a pretence make long prayer: therefore ye shall receive the greater damnation.

Verse 9 therefore makes sense to say…Call none of these (Pharisees) your teachers or your fathers.

The phrase "no man" actually does not have the word "man" in the original text, it can be better understood as "none"

It is similar to **John 10:28-29**

> **John 10:28** And I give unto them eternal life; and they shall never perish, neither shall any man pluck them out of my hand. Vs 29 My Father, which gave them me, is greater than all; and no man is able to pluck them out of my Father's hand.

Man is not the focus, it is anyone or no one.

That said, in simple Bible study you need more than a verse to lay a doctrinal practice.

Scriptural practice is two or three witnesses

> **Matthew 18:16** But if he will not hear thee, then take with thee one or two more, that in the mouth of two or three witnesses every word may be established.

In settling disputes;

1st Corinthians 14:27 If any man speak in an unknown tongue, let it be by two, or at the most by three, and that by course; and let one interpret. Vs 29 Let the prophets speak two or three, and let the other judge.

In judging inspirational gifts of the Spirit;

2nd Corinthians 13:1 This is the third time I am coming to you. In the mouth of two or three witnesses shall every word be established.

So, we should require more than a statement. Besides, we must read the entire Scriptures to see all the contents in a contextual application.

If the verse was meant to mean "Do not call anyone your father", then it is either you are being taught to live in denial or to be disrespectful.

This however is not so, as Jesus did refer to fathers.

Let us examine two or more evidences;

Matthew 19:19 Honour thy father and thy mother: and, Thou shalt love thy neighbour as thyself.

He refers to **Exodus 20:12**, he must be regarding earthly fathers then.

Luke 11:11 If a son shall ask bread of any of you that is a father, will he give him a stone? or if he ask a fish, will he for a fish give him a serpent?

He establishes a relationship of dependence and supply called Father and Son.

Luke 15:11-12 And he said, A certain man had two sons: **Vs 12** And the younger of them said to his father, Father, give me the portion of goods that falleth to me. And he divided unto them his living.

This parable, just like others acknowledges fathers other than God.

In fact, in a certain place He acknowledges the fatherhood rights of the devil.

John 8:44 Ye are of your father the devil, and the lusts of your father ye will do. He was a murderer from the beginning, and abode not in the truth, because there is no truth in him. When he speaketh a lie, he speaketh of his own: for he is a liar, and the father of it.

We can safely say, God is Father to those who have faith in Christ.

John 1:12 But as many as received him, to them

gave he power to become the sons of God, even to them that believe on his name

John 20:17 Jesus saith unto her, Touch me not; for I am not yet ascended to my Father: but go to my brethren, and say unto them, I ascend unto my Father, and your Father; and to my God, and your God.

Men who are responsible for the natural procreation of fellow human beings are scripturally referred to as Fathers too.

The question now lingers, is there any basis for having Spiritual Fathers or Fathers in the Lord (Christ)?

The term Father was translated from the Greek word **"Pater"** in, with several shades of meaning which include

- Nourisher (one who supplies food, sustenance)

- Protector (one who guides and shields)

- Upholder (a helper in perilous times)

- Progenitor (oftentimes used for ancestors). For example in **1ˢᵗ Corinthians 10:1**, **Hebrews 1:1**, it was used for the ancestors of the Jews.

Jesus used the term "Children" also in describing a relationship not in natural terms

> **John 21:5** Then Jesus saith unto them, Children, have ye any meat?

They answered him, No! They were not his natural offspring and historically many were older than him.

Believers were referred to as children of other believers and Fathers consequently and subsequently

Peter did

> **1st Peter 5:13** The Church that is at Babylon, elected together with you , saluteth you; and so doth Marcus my son.

John did

> **3rd John 1:3-4** For I rejoiced greatly, when the brethren came and testified of the truth that is in thee, even as thou walkest in the truth. **Vs 4** I have no greater joy than to hear that my children walk in truth.

Paul did also

> **Galatians 4:19** My little children, of whom I travail in birth again until Christ be formed in you,

This obviously was a well-defined relationship of mentorship, guidance and training. It was not a title. It was a relationship borne out of teaching!

> **2nd Timothy 2:1-2** Thou therefore, my son, be strong in the grace that is in Christ Jesus. **Vs 2** And the things that thou hast heard of me among many witnesses, the same commit thou to faithful men, who shall be able to teach others also.

Paul was responsible for Timothy's doctrinal persuasion.
He was not the preacher when Timothy received Christ. He met him a believer

> **Acts 16:1-3** Then came he to Derbe and Lystra: and, behold, a certain disciple was there, named Timotheus, the son of a certain woman, which was a Jewess, and believed; but his father was a Greek: **Vs 2** Which was well reported of by the brethren that were at Lystra and Iconium. **Vs 3** Him would Paul have to go forth with him; and took and circumcised him because of the Jews which were in those

quarters: for they knew all that his father was a Greek.

Paul acknowledged this.

2nd Timothy 1:5 When I call to remembrance the unfeigned faith that is in thee, which dwelt first in thy grandmother Lois, and thy mother Eunice; and I am persuaded that in thee also.

2nd Timothy 3:15 And that from a child thou hast known the holy Scriptures, which are able to make thee wise unto salvation through faith which is in Christ Jesus.

Yet He was Paul's son by doctrinal persuasion. Also, he (Timothy) was His son by training

Philippians 2:19-22 But I trust in the Lord Jesus to send Timotheus shortly unto you, that I also may be of good comfort, when I know your state. **Vs 20** For I have no man likeminded, who will naturally care for your state. **Vs 21** For all seek their own, not the things which are Jesus Christ's. **Vs 22** But ye know the proof of him, that, as a son with the father, he hath served with me in the gospel.

A Spiritual Father is a trainer. One who builds ministry

into you.

Fathers in the Faith are instructors in Doctrine. They are trainers by example.

> **1st Corinthians 4:15** For though ye have ten thousand instructors in Christ, yet have ye not many fathers: for in Christ Jesus I have begotten you through the gospel.

A father also is someone who invests trust in you.

Especially the fact that He will acknowledge you, endorse you and approve you.

Same way God did for Jesus!

> **Matthew 3:17** And lo a voice from heaven, saying, This is my beloved Son, in whom I am well pleased.

And does for us believers

> **1st John 3:1** Behold, what manner of love the Father hath bestowed upon us, that we should be called the sons of God: therefore the world knoweth us not, because it knew him not.

This was what Paul did for Timothy.

Fathers are givers not takers. Just like our Heavenly Father whom all fathers must mirror.

2nd Corinthians 12:14 Behold, the third time I am ready to come to you; and I will not be burdensome to you: for I seek not yours, but you: for the children ought not to lay up for the parents, but the parents for the children.

They are not to turn this God given privilege to an "anointed" ATM!

1st Peter 5:2 Feed the flock of God which is among you, taking the oversight thereof, not by constraint, but willingly; not for filthy lucre, but of a ready mind;

They must not be seen as lords! But Fathers! Not for filthy lucre or for Money!

Rather for Oversight, care, and exemplary conduct.

Ephesians 6:4 And, ye fathers, provoke not your children to wrath: but bring them up in the nurture and admonition of the Lord.

Fathers are nurturers and not torturers!

It is also very biblical to give financially to anyone responsible for our spiritual upbringing.

Galatians 6:6 Let him that is taught in the word communicate unto him that teacheth in all good things.

Those who teach us the Word, and not prophesy money out of your account

> **1st Timothy 5:17** Let the elders that rule well be counted worthy of double honour, especially they who labour in the word and doctrine. **Vs 18** For the Scripture saith, Thou shalt not muzzle the ox that treadeth out the corn. And, The labourer is worthy of his reward.

Laborers in teaching not one who frequently hires others to do his job or one who rather than stay with the flock to feed and shepherd them junkets around the globe.

> **1st Corinthians 9:11** If we have sown unto you spiritual things, is it a great thing if we shall reap your carnal things? **Vs 14** Even so hath the Lord ordained that they which preach the gospel should live of the gospel.

Spiritual things refer to the ministry of the Word.

However, Fathers do not make demands like;

- You must give me such and such amount to bless you.
- You must put me in Five star hotels etc. Send money to me monthly,

- Can you pay my bills ?

That is no Father. Such men are your sons not and fathers. Since they are the demanding ones! Watch such Debt encouraging relationships. A true Father will remain true.

Helper, Supplier, Succorer, and Teacher! It is apt to note as earlier said, this term only describes relationships ongoing.

You do not look for a Spiritual Father. You only discover who it has been all along!

Many have been blackmailed into manipulative associations.

Who is your spiritual father? If you say "am not sure", you are immediately classed as - independent minded and unsubmissive...

That is unscriptural!

The basis is for a believer to be accountable to other believers, and this is Primary in a Local assembly.

Ephesians 5:21 Submitting yourselves one to another in the fear of God.

Hebrews 10:25 Not forsaking the assembling of

ourselves together, as the manner of some is; but exhorting one another: and so much the more, as ye see the day approaching.

Paul submitted to other believers (ministers) even though they didn't teach similar things.

> **Galatians 2:2** And I went up by revelation, and communicated unto them that gospel which I preach among the Gentiles, but privately to them which were of reputation, lest by any means I should run, or had run, in vain.

That is basic. Have a local Church. Have a pastor, Ministers with whom you relate with and are accountable to. If along the way, you discover who your Spiritual Father is, blessed are You.

If you do not, your Father; the Father of our Lord Jesus Christ; the Father of Lights (as we are His lights), remaineth still!

SHOULD I FOLLOW MEN?

"Stop following a man, follow Christ!"

This phrase is often said at or to folks who seem overly committed to a preacher or Church.

The question however, is Christian living possible without following men?

Let us visit revealed Scriptures for clarity of thought.

2ⁿᵈ Timothy 3:16 All Scripture is given by inspiration of God, and is profitable for doctrine, for reproof, for correction, for instruction in righteousness:

The entire Scriptures were written about men.

The writer of Hebrews puts in a succinct manner.

Hebrews 11:2 For by it the elders obtained a good report.

The entire Old Testament books of the Bible is the good report; report of men. Hence, the whole chapters, more pungent Scriptures were written by men.

2ⁿᵈ Peter 1:21 For the prophecy came not in old time by the will of man: but holy men of God spake as they were moved by the Holy Ghost.

Men wrote it!

From Moses:

John 1:17 For the law was given by Moses, but grace and truth came by Jesus Christ.

John 5:46 For had ye believed Moses, ye would have believed me: for he wrote of me.

In fact, he gained enormous weight in so much as an era was accorded him.

1st Corinthians 10:2 And were all baptized unto Moses in the cloud and in the sea;

This was a man; Moses.

The savior is also a man at His incarnation.

John 1:14 And the Word was made flesh, and dwelt among us, (and we beheld his glory, the glory as of the only begotten of the Father,) full of grace and truth.

He is still a man after his resurrection.

1st Timothy 2:5 For there is one God, and one mediator between God and men, the man Christ Jesus;

Again,

His mandate to reach the world was committed to men.

Matthew 28:18 And Jesus came and spake unto them, saying, All power is given unto me in heaven and in earth. **Vs 19** Go ye therefore, and teach all nations, baptizing them in the name of the Father, and of the Son, and of the Holy Ghost: **Vs 20** Teaching them to observe all things whatsoever I have commanded you: and, lo, I am with you alway, even unto the end of the world. Amen.

They are to make disciples.

> **Mark 16:15** And he said unto them, Go ye into all the world, and preach the gospel to every creature.

Preach Him.

> **John 20:21** Then said Jesus to them again, Peace be unto you: as my Father hath sent me, even so send I you… **Vs 23** Whose soever sins ye remit, they are remitted unto them; and whose soever sins ye retain, they are retained.

That is such enormous responsibility and authority given to men.

> **Acts 1:8** But ye shall receive power, after that the Holy Ghost is come upon you: and ye shall be witnesses unto me both in Jerusalem, and in all Judaea, and in Samaria, and unto the uttermost part of the earth.

Men are to be His witnesses. Since he is in heaven, we see Him in men and hear Him in men. Men will minister the things and gifts of the Spirit to others.

> **Acts 8:15** Who, when they were come down, prayed

for them, that they might receive the Holy Ghost... **Vs 17** Then laid they their hands on them, and they received the Holy Ghost.

Men made men receive.

Acts 9:17 And Ananias went his way, and entered into the house; and putting his hands on him said, Brother Saul, the Lord, even Jesus, that appeared unto thee in the way as thou camest, hath sent me, that thou mightest receive thy sight, and be filled with the Holy Ghost.

Ananias made Paul receive.

Acts 10:44 While Peter yet spake these words, the Holy Ghost fell on all them which heard the word.

This happened as Peter spoke.

Acts 19:6 And when Paul had laid his hands upon them, the Holy Ghost came on them; and they spake with tongues, and prophesied.

Paul laid his hands on men and the Holy Ghost came.

Ministry is also received this way.

Acts 13:2 As they ministered to the Lord, and fasted,

the Holy Ghost said, Separate me Barnabas and Saul for the work whereunto I have called them.

Men said this by utterances.

Acts 13:3 And when they had fasted and prayed, and laid their hands on them, they sent them away. **Vs 4** So they, being sent forth by the Holy Ghost, departed unto Seleucia; and from thence they sailed to Cyprus.

Men sent them away and the Holy Ghost did.

Paul reminded Timothy.

1st Timothy 4:14 Neglect not the gift that is in thee, which was given thee by prophecy, with the laying on of the hands of the presbytery. **Vs 6** Wherefore I put thee in remembrance that thou stir up the gift of God, which is in thee by the putting on of my hands.

Spiritual growth is made available via men who bring us up.

Acts 2:42 And they continued stedfastly in the apostles' doctrine and fellowship, and in breaking of bread, and in prayers.

Apostles are men. They were devoted to the apostles'

teaching. You will see that through the book of Acts,

Acts 5:42 And daily in the temple, and in every house, they ceased not to teach and preach Jesus Christ.

No one tried to know God by himself. They knew him via men he sent to them.

> **Acts 11:26** And when he had found him, he brought him unto Antioch. And it came to pass, that a whole year they assembled themselves with the Church, and taught much people. And the disciples were called Christians first in Antioch.

Same here.

> **Acts 19:8** And he went into the synagogue, and spake boldly for the space of three months, disputing and persuading the things concerning the kingdom of God. **Vs 9** But when divers were hardened, and believed not, but spake evil of that way before the multitude, he departed from them, and separated the disciples, disputing daily in the school of one Tyrannus. **Vs 10** And this continued by the space of two years; so that all they which dwelt in Asia heard the word of the Lord Jesus, both Jews and Greeks.

And here,

Acts 20:20 And how I kept back nothing that was profitable unto you , but have shewed you, and have taught you publicly, and from house to house,

Paul put it aptly.

1ˢᵗ Corinthians 14:36 What? came the word of God out from you? or came it unto you only?

The Word did not come from you but unto you. God gave men.

Ephesians 4:8 Wherefore he saith, When he ascended up on high, he led captivity captive, and gave gifts unto men… **Vs 11** And he gave some, apostles; and some, prophets; and some, evangelists; and some, pastors and teachers; **Vs 12** For the perfecting of the saints, for the work of the ministry, for the edifying of the body of Christ: **Vs 13** Till we all come in the unity of the faith, and of the knowledge of the Son of God, unto a perfect man, unto the measure of the stature of the fulness of Christ: **Vs 14** That we henceforth be no more children, tossed to and fro, and carried about with every wind of doctrine, by the sleight of men, and cunning craftiness, whereby they lie in wait to deceive;

He achieves His work through men. You cannot grow by yourself.

Colossians 1:28 Whom we preach, warning every man, and teaching every man in all wisdom; that we may present every man perfect in Christ Jesus:

Men will make you perfect, matured in Christ.

Galatians 4:19 My little children, of whom I travail in birth again until Christ be formed in you,

Men do this. Thus, we are taught in Scriptures to follow men! Esteem them highly.

1st Thessalonians 5:12 And we beseech you, brethren, to know them which labour among you, and are over you in the Lord, and admonish you; **Vs 13** And to esteem them very highly in love for their work's sake. And be at peace among yourselves.

We cannot grow if we do not. Esteem highly means to exalt above all men.

Hebrews 13:17 Obey them that have the rule over you, and submit yourselves: for they watch for your souls, as they that must give account, that they may do it with joy, and not with grief: for that is unprofitable for you.

We obey them; submit ourselves. Else, we shall be blamed of God. They are responsible for our lives.

1ˢᵗ Corinthians 4:16 Wherefore I beseech you, be ye followers of me.

We are to follow men. That is how we follow Christ.

Some have been more mischievous. They misquote Paul. They say "follow men as they follow Christ". This is not in Scriptures. At least, Paul did not write it.

1ˢᵗ Corinthians 11:1 Be ye followers of me, even as I also am of Christ.

The word "also" is italicized. Hence, it is explained as "Follow even as I am of Christ".

Therefore, you are to follow him because he is of Christ.

That is consistent with all his other counsels. We know Christ and follow him via men.

Some also misquote John:

1ˢᵗ John 2:27 But the anointing which ye have received of him abideth in you, and ye need not that any man teach you: but as the same anointing teacheth you of all things, and is truth, and is no lie, and even as it hath taught you, ye shall abide in him.

The writer is a man.

We actually follow men if we are truly following Christ. This is just like we serve men if we are truly serving Christ.

What exactly are we to follow?

Teaching !

2nd Timothy 3:10 But thou hast fully known my doctrine, manner of life, purpose, faith, longsuffering, charity, patience, **Vs 14** But continue thou in the things which thou hast learned and hast been assured of, knowing of whom thou hast learned them ;l Faith ,patience ,virtues. Not kind of car, house, favorite colours, chosen career.

In Greek construction, the word "doctrine" is followed by semicolon in today's grammar. All others are from his teaching.

Faith is used many times in Paul's letters to Timothy for doctrine and lifestyle.

1st Timothy 6:12 Fight the good fight of faith, lay

hold on eternal life, whereunto thou art also called, and hast professed a good profession before many witnesses.

2ⁿᵈ Timothy 4:7 I have fought a good fight, I have finished my course, I have kept the faith:

Writer of Hebrews also counseled,

Hebrews 13:7 Remember them which have the rule over you, who have spoken unto you the word of God: whose faith follow, considering the end of their conversation.

Notice again the sequence …whose faith follow.

They are human beings like you whom God is using for you. However, they make mistakes too. "Flawed men", that is all that God has at his disposal!

The treasure is in weak vessels

2ⁿᵈ Corinthians 4:7 But we have this treasure in earthen vessels, that the excellency of the power may be of God, and not of us.

It is the beauty of grace. Flawed men ministering the power of God; teaching Christ, the flawless person.

1st Corinthians 2:1 And I, brethren, when I came to you, came not with excellency of speech or of wisdom, declaring unto you the testimony of God. **Vs 2** For I determined not to know any thing among you, save Jesus Christ, and him crucified.

We shall learn of the person of Christ from and through them.

2nd Corinthians 4:5 For we preach not ourselves, but Christ Jesus the Lord; and ourselves your servants for Jesus' sake.

We shall follow him through them. We shall grow in him through them.

That is the wisdom of God; to hear God, hear them; to learn of Him, hear them; to follow Him, follow men.

That is all God's got and all you and I have too.

SHOULD I FOLLOW MEN? (2)

Growing up as a believer within what we referred to then as "conservative Christianity" was the pursuit to imitate Christ.

In the very words of Paul,

1st Corinthians 11:1 Be ye followers of me, even as I also am of Christ.

However, later emerged the teaching usually termed "motivation" where a mantra soon hit the airwaves, "Dare To Be Different" with much more psychological embellishments like "no one has your fingerprints" etc. This is kind of funny as it is no revelation.

We dumped clear apostolic instruction,

Philippians 2:2 Fulfil ye my joy, that ye be likeminded, having the same love, being of one accord, of one mind. **Vs 5** Let this mind be in you, which was also in Christ Jesus:

We hardly realize this birth divisions beyond the ordinary and formed the basis of the conundrum in Corinth.

1st Corinthians 1:11 For it hath been declared unto me of you, my brethren, by them which are of the house of Chloe, that there are contentions among you. **Vs 12** Now this I say, that every one of you saith, I am of Paul; and I of Apollos; and I of Cephas; and I of Christ.

The apostles had a different testimony.

Acts 4:13 Now when they saw the boldness of Peter and John, and perceived that they were unlearned and ignorant men, they marvelled; and they took knowledge of them, that they had been with Jesus.

They reflected just one person - Christ.

That said,

My main issue for discourse here is how many younger preachers have been thus compelled by this "express yourself", "your own thing", "your own message", inspiration which has amounted to them severing supernatural relationships.

During a workers and leaders session in my local Church where I serve as pastor, I had the cause to speak along these same lines.

I said "you are already different; your name, background, likes, dislikes, clubs you support, kind of spouse you chose, career path, very unique experiences etc. This will definitely reflect in your personality." I actually with humor demonstrated some peculiar nuances with many reeling with laughter.

This is rather auspicious.

With our different personalities, we are not permitted to have different beliefs. Our message must align with each other as saying the same thing.

All the Old Testament prophets had the same message.

> **Luke 24:25** Then he said unto them, O fools, and slow of heart to believe all that the prophets have spoken: **Vs 26** Ought not Christ to have suffered these things, and to enter into his glory? **Vs 27** And beginning at Moses and all the prophets, he expounded unto them in all the Scriptures the things concerning himself… **Vs 44** And he said unto them, These are the words which I spake unto you, while I was yet with you, that all things must be fulfilled, which were written in the law of Moses, and in the prophets, and in the psalms, concerning me.

All ministers of the gospel must have the same message even though depths and explanation might vary.

> **Ephesians 4:5** One Lord, one faith, one baptism, **Vs 6** One God and Father of all, who is above all, and through all, and in you all. **Vs 13** Till we all come in the unity of the faith, and of the knowledge of the Son of God, unto a perfect man, unto the measure of the stature of the fulness of Christ:

Paul instructed Timothy to ensure this

> **1ˢᵗ Timothy 1:3** As I besought thee to abide still at Ephesus, when I went into Macedonia, that thou mightest charge some that they teach no other doctrine,

Hence, I detest the use of the term "I do not agree or I disagree" on doctrinal issues. It is either "I have not seen it" or "I have not understood it" or "it is not true in Scriptures" or "it is true".

Hear peter

> **2ⁿᵈ Peter 3:16** As also in all his epistles, speaking in them of these things; in which are some things hard to be understood, which they that are unlearned and unstable wrest, as they do also the other Scriptures, unto their own destruction.

Understanding was the issue, not subject to agreeing or otherwise.

In finding and discovering spiritual fathers / mentors, we must be particular about doctrine.

> **2ⁿᵈ Timothy 2:1** Thou therefore, my son, be strong in the grace that is in Christ Jesus. **Vs 2** And the things that thou hast heard of me among many witnesses, the same commit thou to faithful men,

who shall be able to teach others also.

The same!

However, "the same" will not be taught by the "same personalities".

Many in the quest to assert their personalities and dare to be different have gone after strange revelations. They assume people need to hear their own revelation. They think that it is not a good image to be found saying the same thing as another. Many break away out of this ego to found ministries and Churches, daring to be different! Oftentimes, it leads from one error to another.

I have seen some use our ministry materials to build teachings and try to add to or take away, edit or re-package the same. Hence, they will not be found out by their followers to be following our ministry!

2ⁿᵈ Corinthians 10:12 For we dare not make ourselves of the number, or compare ourselves with some that commend themselves: but they measuring themselves by themselves, and comparing themselves among themselves, are not wise.

All of us do quote from writers of Scripture! I also follow people too. Hence, it is very scriptural and healthy to follow. There is nothing odd in saying exactly what your pastor/mentor says all the time, since it is Scripture. The truth is that you will always say it your own way since your personality is different.

You should not go away from God's will for your life as touching supernatural relationships because of ego.

It is healthy to find someone whose teachings you can adopt and adapt to perfectly.

Timothy found his.

However, one thing is clear; your experiences will be unique. It always is.

Joshua followed Moses. He was his son.

> **Deuteronomy 34:9** And Joshua the son of Nun was full of the spirit of wisdom; for Moses had laid his hands upon him: and the children of Israel hearkened unto him, and did as the Lord commanded Moses.

Joshua's ministry was Moses'. However, he had his own uniqueness. He stopped the earth from rotating. God said that He never hearkened to any man like Joshua. Moses used the rod to part the sea, Joshua had the people cross Jordan without the rod. Whilst Moses asked the spies to address the congregation, Joshua learnt from it and asked them to speak with him first lest they spread doubt as they did in **Numbers 13 &14**.

This was the same with Elijah and Elisha. Elisha's ministry was Elijah's.

Earlier on he served him,

> **2ⁿᵈ Kings 3:1** But Jehoshaphat said, Is there not here a prophet of the Lord , that we may enquire of the Lord by him? And one of the king of Israel's servants answered and said, Here is Elisha the son of Shaphat, which poured water on the hands of Elijah.

He poured water. Hence, everyone knew him.

Just like Joshua to Moses, we had Timothy to Paul,

> **Philippians 2:20** For I have no man likeminded, who will naturally care for your state **Vs 21** For all seek their own, not the things which are Jesus Christ's. **Vs 22** But ye know the proof of him, that, as a son with the father, he hath served with me in the gospel.

He served Paul; he was his boy. Everyone knew this.

Same as Elisha, he purportedly wore his mantle. This was despite the fact that Elisha had a different background. He was older in age, had a wealthy background such that he had to let go.

1st Kings 19:19 So he departed thence, and found Elisha the son of Shaphat, who was plowing with twelve yoke of oxen before him, and he with the twelfth: and Elijah passed by him, and cast his mantle upon him.

Hence, his ministry bore his personality. He ministered Elisha's ministry with his own uniqueness. He was not trying to be different.

In fact, he was seen as Elijah.

2nd Kings 2:15 And when the sons of the prophets which were to view at Jericho saw him, they said, The spirit of Elijah doth rest on Elisha. And they came to meet him, and bowed themselves to the ground before him.

There is no need to try to break away, wear it with pride.

Also, we had David and Solomon. We can go on and on.

Do not stray from God's plan because you want to be unique. It is believed that Barnabas was called to follow Paul. However, ego got in the way and we never hear of him again. It is not as if his ministry ended. The moment you are striving to be seen and known, something is out of place.

A fellow wanted to leave a Church and I asked him "why?" "Is the teaching different from Scriptures and yours?"

He said "no". I asked "were you given the ability to oversee there?" He said yes. Are you planning to start a Church? He said yes. I asked "Why, since it is the same thing that you are already doing here you want to do when you leave?

I was miffed because he just wanted to be his own man!

Soon enough he will not want to be seen copying the said Pastor. He will try to introduce his own "revs". Off he goes, another doctrinal catastrophe in the making! This is simply because he could not stomach copying another. He might even have cheer leaders urging him on as Rehoboam and Ahithophel in Scriptures or those who tried to steer David off course.

> **1st Samuel 18:7** And the women answered one another as they played, and said, Saul hath slain his thousands, and David his ten thousands.

David only killed one person.

We might yield to such folks and see it as an

abomination to be seen copying another in order to please our fans.

Watch it the next time anyone tells you to be different.

You already are!

THE MINISTER AND THE LOCAL CHURCH

How to Find a Local Church & Stay Committed There

The local Church refers to a gathering of believers in a particular location and is a part of the universal Church, the body of Christ which consists of believers in every part of the world (**Romans 12:5, 1ˢᵗ Corinthians 12:12, Ephesians 2:12**).

Finding a local Church, as simple as it may sound requires the wisdom of God's word and so does getting and staying committed there.

The issue will not be to locate the venue of one, especially since there's almost one or two on every street nowadays.

Deciding on which local Church to identify with is a serious matter and should be done PRAYERFULLY AND PURPOSEFULLY.

Its closeness to your place of residence, a common consideration with many people today would be unwise, because many travel sometimes all the way abroad to study or to get medical attention, which is an indication of a desire for the best available, therefore the same attitude should be employed for something as important and eternal as locating a Church to attend.

If you take your Christian life seriously, you should choose to attend the best local Church around you.

While it's easy to get carried away by GOOD MUSIC, SHORT MESSAGE SERVICE (SMS) AND NICE LOOKING USHERS and FIRST TIMER GIFTS AND FOOD PACKS.

Some are even carried away by activities, they are not learning the word of God or growing up spiritually in the Church - they play the keyboard, the drums, are in drama group etc.

They would rather be involved in activities than grow up spiritually. Others still are in a particular Church because "It's our family Church", "my friends are in the Church" or "I have connections there".

All these considerations though may make sense to the carnal man, have no spiritual benefit.

Before you choose a local Church, ask yourself these questions:

1. DO I WANT TO GROW SPIRITUALLY?

If yes, then you must choose to attend a local Church where the teaching of God's word is given first place and every member is closely mentored and monitored to understand every Bible doctrine.

WHY? Because spiritual growth will only come with

growth in the knowledge of God's word-Jesus Christ **(John 1:1-5, 9-16, 1Peter 2:2, Acts 20:20)**.

Spiritual growth will come by the revelation of who Jesus is, all he has done for us and all we can do because we are in Him (Colossians 1:9, Ephesians 1:19, 3:16-19, Philemon 6).

2. DO YOU WANT TO CONSISTENTLY SEE GOD'S DIVINE HAND IN ALL YOUR AFFAIRS IN LIFE?

If yes!

Then you must attend a local Church where a lot of time is devoted to prayer and particularly praying in the spirit (in tongues)

WHY?

Because prayer is a demonstration of our trust in and our dependence upon God.

By prayer, great power; God's power is made available for everyone in life situations and circumstances, thus the Bible teaches us to pray fervently **(James 5:16)** and to pray always in the spirit **(Ephesians 6:18)** praying in the spirit is praying in tongues (**1 Corinthians 14:2, 4, 15, 18, Jude 20**).

3. DO YOU WANT TO WALK IN THE WILL OF GOD FOR YOUR LIFE?

If yes again!

Then you must choose a local Church that is in the will of God.

And how can you tell? It must be a local Church where EVANGELISM and reaching the lost is not treated with levity or taken as a pastime but, is approached with a deep sense of purpose and responsibility and is received, as a commission of JESUS CHRIST, the head of the Church (**Matthew 28:18-20, Mark 16:15-20**).

WHY?
Staying in the will of God for your life starts with obeying God in general instructions and paying attention to light in His word with which comes more specific instructions (**Romans 12:2**).

4. DO YOU WANT TO LIVE FAR ABOVE THE FORCES OF DARKNESS OF THE WORLD?

Again if Yes!

Excitedly so! Then you must attend a local Church where there's an atmosphere of LOVE, JOY AND FAITH IN GOD'S WORD.
WHY?
Because the system of this world is ruled by the god of this world, the devil (**2nd Corinthians 4:4, Ephesians**

2:2).

The believer will only win in life all the time by putting on the whole armour of GOD (**Ephesians 6:10-18**)

How is that Possible? **1st John 5:4**

> **1st John 5:4** For whatsoever is born of God overcometh the world: and this is the victory that overcometh the world, *even* our faith.

5. DO YOU WANT TO BE A BLESSING TO OTHERS AND FLOW WITH THE GIFTS OF THE SPIRIT?

Sure Yes!

Then you must attend a local Church where room is given to each one to express things of and things pertaining to the Spirit, tongues, interpretation of tongues, prophecies, amongst others (**1st Corinthians 14:12-15**).

WHY!

Because things of the Spirit will only improve with practice (**1st Corinthians 12:31, 14:39, Hebrews 5:14**).

Staying committed to this local Church must be with the

understanding that the local Church is God's plan for the believer, a place where he has a pastor who teaches and trains him spiritually, who is responsible to bring to him correction, reproof, and instructions in righteousness (**2nd Timothy 3:16**).

The local Church therefore has spiritual leaders who have Christ's authority to lead you (**Hebrews 13:7**) and your response to them must thus be submission in love and obedience as unto God (**Hebrews 13:17**).

Dear Pastor (young minister), what are you doing in His House?

The Church is not an all-purpose, multilateral avenue which can be turned into a daycare center, business school, political campaign center, cooking school, nation building center, driving school etc. all in the name of meeting needs.

Jesus warned about this.

> **Mark 11:17** And he taught, saying unto them, Is it not written, My house shall be called of all nations the house of prayer? but ye have made it a den of thieves.

It is a house of prayer; spiritual activities.

Jesus exemplified that straightaway.

> **Mark 11:15** And they come to Jerusalem: and Jesus went into the temple, and began to cast out them that sold and bought in the temple, and overthrew the tables of the moneychangers, and the seats of them that sold doves; **Vs 16** And would not suffer that any man should carry any vessel through the

temple.

He chased out those organizing entrepreneurship seminars, selling shares, multi-level marketing, branding, and project management. He chased them and TAUGHT. That is what His house is for!

There is nothing wrong in business seminars, deals etc. for believers. It is good and noble, but not in His house. It is not why God placed you as pastor. Hence, stop the abuse of your office.

John's account was more graphic.

> **John 2:15** And when he had made a scourge of small cords, he drove them all out of the temple, and the sheep, and the oxen; and poured out the changers' money, and overthrew the tables;

He used a cane!

Does this mean that believers do not need to make money, build business empires and careers?

Truth is that is not the work of the Church or Pastor.

Your Pastor does not repair your car, choose your house design, become tutorial teacher for you in school, teach you how to have sex with your spouse, diagnose sickness and disease, teach you how to dress up etc.!

God did not give pastors the gifts of the Spirit to compete with business schools, banks, hospitals and universities.

It is a needless waste of time and resources.

> **Ephesians 4:11** And he gave some, apostles; and some, prophets; and some, evangelists; and some, pastors and teachers; **Vs 12** For the perfecting of the saints, for the work of the ministry, for the edifying of the body of Christ: **Vs 13** Till we all come in the unity of the faith, and of the knowledge of the Son of God, unto a perfect man, unto the measure of the stature of the fulness of Christ: **Vs 14** That we henceforth be no more children, tossed to and fro, and carried about with every wind of doctrine, by the sleight of men, and cunning craftiness, whereby they lie in wait to deceive;

This is not till we all become great politicians, become featured in Forbes or Fortune 500! Get your acts right.

Whilst it is needful to cater for the welfare of members who are in physical needs like food and shelter, turning the Church into a commercial center is an error.

Some have mischievously said Jesus taught about business etc. Jesus was not teaching commerce in the parable of talents or rather was he making a reference to it whilst teaching the gospel. He was not teaching agriculture in the parable of the sower nor was he using it as illustrations.

They were illustrations not subjects on their own just like Paul was not teaching anatomy and physiology in **1st Corinthians 12**.

By the way, he used illustrations for the non-believer and spiritually blind.

> **Matthew 13:13** Therefore speak I to them in parables: because they seeing see not; and hearing they hear not, neither do they understand.

> **Matthew 13:34** All these things spake Jesus unto the multitude in parables; and without a parable spake he not unto them: **Vs 35** That it might be fulfilled which was spoken by the prophet, saying, I will open my mouth in parables; I will utter things which have been kept secret from the foundation of the world.

I realize many upcoming ministers are catching this bug. They are trying to grow the Church at all costs. They do not want members going elsewhere for this, when they actually should. Otherwise, we shall succeed in breeding more unserious believers.

In reality, no serious businessman will rely on your

Church growth strategy seminar for real business.

Note Paul's warning:

> **1st Corinthians 3:10** According to the grace of God which is given unto me, as a wise master builder, I have laid the foundation, and another buildeth thereon. But let every man take heed how he buildeth thereupon **Vs 11** For other foundation can no man lay than that is laid, which is Jesus Christ **Vs 12** Now if any man build upon this foundation gold, silver, precious stones, wood, hay, stubble; **Vs 13** Every man's work shall be made manifest: for the day shall declare it, because it shall be revealed by fire; and the fire shall try every man's work of what sort it is. **Vs 14** If any man's work abide which he hath built thereupon, he shall receive a reward.

Please build spiritual things, eternal things.

Learn from what the apostles said.

> **Acts 6:2** Then the twelve called the multitude of the disciples unto them , and said, It is not reason that we should leave the word of God, and serve tables. **Vs 4** But we will give ourselves continually to prayer, and to the ministry of the word.

Dear pastor, know this:

Succeeding in God's plan is not getting involved in every matter but sticking to and doing what really matters.

Like Paul,

> **2nd Timothy 4:7** I have fought a good fight, I have finished my course, I have kept the faith:

"The faith" refers to the message, the doctrine. That is what really matters. Keep it, preserve it and teach it.

Do not get moved by vogues.

Remember his counsel to Timothy.

> **1st Timothy 3:15** But if I tarry long, that thou mayest know how thou oughtest to behave thyself in the house of God, which is the Church of the living God, the pillar and ground of the truth.

Feed the flock

> **John 21:16** He saith to him again the second time, Simon, son of Jonas, lovest thou me? He saith unto him, Yea, Lord; thou knowest that I love thee. He saith unto him, Feed my sheep.

The term "feed" means oversight, care, support and attention.

A pastor must accept that his work demands concentration on the flock. Flock refers to a people specific. Only Jesus oversees the Body of Christ. Every pastor has his own field whilst he is yet available to the body of Christ. He must know his primary assignment is the local Church.

> **Acts 20:28** Take heed therefore unto yourselves, and to all the flock, over the which the Holy Ghost hath made you overseers, to feed the Church of God, which he hath purchased with his own blood.

A pastor must take heed to the flock God gave him to oversee. He must be seen attending to it primarily.

Before I started to serve as Pastor of Saints Community Church in 2007, I had several other pastoral exposures either in acting capacity, assistant capacity or at times in full capacity over 11-12 years. Before then, many of those times, I was growing in my understanding of what it means to pastor.

I loved travelling. I remember having to hitchhike across four (4) African nations in 1996 to preach.

My first visit outside Nigeria was late November 1994 to Ghana to hold a Bible Seminar and later a Crusade. I travelled by night.

I have been to communities to minister where no one spoke our language. I just loved going round and round, I travelled to thirty four (34) states of the nation (Nigeria) visiting different villages, towns and cities. In one single year, we were at fifty- five (55) campuses asides several Churches and denominations. We had Crusades, Holy Ghost meetings, teaching seminars etc.

Interestingly, in the midst of all these, I had Churches I was meant to pastor or assist etc. Obviously, I was not taking heed to the flock!

How can you be away from your local Church so many times in the year?

You must identify who, where and what your primary assignment is.

> **1st Thessalonians 5:12** And we beseech you, brethren, to know them which labour among you, and are over you in the Lord, and admonish you; **Vs**

13 And to esteem them very highly in love for their work's sake. And be at peace among yourselves.

The term "among you" shows he was referring to a specific people.

No one is sent to superintend the body of Christ but the local Churches have specific superintendents.

These men must attend to the flock. They must be around and available; be found taking the teaching themselves, holding workers training, attending to the needs of the people.

Some are mere executive pastors, just titles. This ought not to be so.

> **1st Timothy 5:17** Let the elders that rule well be counted worthy of double honour, especially they who labour in the word and doctrine.

The emphasis is on those who labor in teaching and preaching.

This admonition was for Timothy, specifically for the local Church he superintends.

> **2nd Timothy 2:2** And the things that thou hast heard of me among many witnesses, the same commit thou to faithful men, who shall be able to teach others also.

That is, to teach others in the congregation.

> **1st Peter 5:2** Feed the flock of God which is among you, taking the oversight thereof, not by constraint, but willingly; not for filthy lucre, but of a ready mind;

Peters says the same, that is, to feed the flock AMONG you, not the Church in the universe.

Some hardly stay in their local Church even though they are called its "pastor". They are always on the road attending to others duties. Some, because of money, ambition and fame or better still quick material success abandon the flock, maybe because it is small in number, so they travel around. That is a hireling.

In all my years of traveling, I hardly took honorariums.

Note that it is not wrong.

> **1st Corinthians 9:14** Even so hath the Lord ordained that they which preach the gospel should live of the gospel.

It was just my choice. This was because I worked for a living outside preaching. Most times, I pay my way there and even handle my hotel bills.

That said,

If you must pastor, stay with the flock; feed the flock.

This means to be seen, heard, watched and learnt under frequently. If you must travel, do so carefully and circumspectly. Spend less time outside your local Church. If more pastors did this, we would develop more stable and sound believers, more ministers would be developed.

When you invite twenty preachers for a three day event as some do, you cannot build a local Church on visiting ministers! Such people usually are not well discipled!

> **Ephesians 4:14** That we henceforth be no more children, tossed to and fro, and carried about with every wind of doctrine, by the sleight of men, and cunning craftiness, whereby they lie in wait to deceive;

Too many believers are like this.

I have had the cause to counsel pastors who want me to speak for them so often. I tell them, "you will do a better job than me over your local Church". You listen to me via recorded materials etc. Go back to your Church and teach it in your own words, your style and your mode. You are their Pastor NOT me. While I can come occasionally, they are your duty not mine!

I hardly take an invitation on a Sunday, Wednesday (during our weekly meetings) or even when I have to lecture in our training school. This is because you do not get an award for helping other people's homes whilst yours is in a mess.

The man of God should stay with the flock, watch it grow; endure the pains, times, stress. He should watch the flock mature.

Hoopla about Family ministries

"What is the Church turning to?"

This was angrily said by a Facebook commentary titan. "Imagine the man is now handing over the leadership of the Church to his son", he went on and on till I had to privately educate him. "This is not politics sir", I told him, "your opinion does not count here, Scriptures do.

Each case must be seen with and in its own merits. You cannot make such comments without proper investigation and dismissing the successor (son of the leader) without checking his antecedents and see whether he is fit for the leadership scripturally.

God put choosing leaders within our purview and as led by His spirit, in agreement with Scriptures.

"There is no need getting worked up sir", I told him. Therefore, I took him through Scriptures and he calmed down and put down the post he put out.

Hence, as believers, we must know our boundaries.

A popular adage in my tribe (Yoruba) says "when a dog goes rabid, it must yet respect its owner.

Thus, respect the Church and its Head; Jesus, its leaders and above all, the Scriptures.

This is not up for debate like national issues. If you cannot study Scriptures, allow those who do, comment on strictly Bible matters. This issue is strictly Scriptures, there is no democracy here.

That said,

Sentiments hardly interpret things appropriately; emotions are usually terrible judges.

> **James 1:19** Wherefore, my beloved brethren, let every man be swift to hear, slow to speak, slow to wrath: **Vs 20** For the wrath of man worketh not the righteousness of God.

Our judgment of persons and issues must be with caution and wisdom. We must never be acting on what journalists write. Most of the media are motivated by Satan and are not promoting the cause of the gospel.

That said,

Is it scriptural for families to run ministries together, that is, husband and wife with children also involved and inclusive?

First and foremost, it is not a requirement nor does it have to be the norm.

Ephesians 4:8 Wherefore he saith, When he ascended up on high, he led captivity captive, and gave gifts unto men.

He gave gifts to men not families.

However, neither is it unscriptural to have natural families or those with natural ties head ministries.

The basic requirements for Church leadership are sacrosanct.

Outlined in Paul's letters to Timothy,

1st Timothy 3:1 This is a true saying, If a man desire the office of a bishop, he desireth a good work.

And His letter to Titus,

Titus 1:5 For this cause left I thee in Crete, that thou shouldest set in order the things that are wanting, and ordain elders in every city, as I had appointed thee:

In no place, does he say "you must ensure a man heads the Church with his wife and kids and they must be his successors when he passes to glory". Also, neither will you find "never allow anyone lead a Church with his family, God so detests it".

Historically, callings and ministries have been perpetuated within families. Abraham, Isaac and Jacob were all God's prophets and succeeded each other; Aaron and Levites (sons of Levi, Aaron inclusive); David, Solomon etc.

We should take note that these were not the only happenstances. Other scenarios did exist. Families did lead ministries and also succeeded each other.

Now let us get nearer.

> **Hebrews 7:9** And as I may so say, Levi also, who receiveth tithes, payed tithes in Abraham.

Levi is a family.

> **Hebrews 11:9** By faith he sojourned in the land of promise, as in a strange country, dwelling in tabernacles with Isaac and Jacob, the heirs with him of the same promise:

Abraham, Isaac and Jacob.

Let us come closer in history.

Amongst Jesus' disciples were blood brothers.

> **Matthew 10:2** Now the names of the twelve apostles are these; The first, Simon, who is called Peter, and Andrew his brother; James the son of Zebedee, and John his brother;

Amongst the apostles was Jesus half-brother too (though some needless try to dispute this).

Galatians 1:19 But other of the apostles saw I none, save James the Lord's brother.

1ˢᵗ Corinthians 15:7 After that, he was seen of James; then of all the apostles.

He was mentioned in the four gospels but not as a disciple.

Mark 6:3 Is not this the carpenter, the son of Mary, the brother of James..

Matthew 13:55 Is not this the carpenter's son? is not his mother called Mary? and his brethren, James,

He led the Church at Jerusalem.

Acts 15:13 And after they had held their peace, James answered, saying, Men and brethren, hearken unto me:

This was not the James who was an apostle in the four gospels.

Acts 12:2 And he killed James the brother of John with the sword.

He had been murdered (martyred) earlier by Herod.

He played prominent roles.

> **Acts 21:18** And the day following Paul went in with us unto James; and all the elders were present.

He led the major / mother Church assembly in the world then.

In fact, he wrote the earliest epistle.

> **James 1:1** James, a servant of God and of the Lord Jesus Christ, to the twelve tribes which are scattered abroad, greeting.

He was regarded severally as the Lord's brother. If you truly believe in the humanity of Jesus, he really was his earthly brother.

There are other examples of families leading and overseeing Churches.

Before this, let us not forget whole families and households did receive the gospel and even together.

> **Acts 11:14** Who shall tell thee words, whereby thou and all thy house shall be saved.

Cornelius' household got saved.

Same as the jailer,

> **Acts 16:34** And when he had brought them into his

house, he set meat before them, and rejoiced, believing in God with all his house.

Now,

Let us consider ministries.

Priscilla and Aquila were a married couple.

> **Acts 18:2** And found a certain Jew named Aquila, born in Pontus, lately come from Italy, with his wife Priscilla; (because that Claudius had commanded all Jews to depart from Rome:) and came unto them… **Vs 26** And he began to speak boldly in the synagogue: whom when Aquila and Priscilla had heard, they took him unto them , and expounded unto him the way of God more perfectly.

They functioned in ministry together. It even appeared from the construction of texts that Priscilla was more prominent. They led the Church as a couple.

> **1st Corinthians 16:19** The Churches of Asia salute you. Aquila and Priscilla salute you much in the Lord, with the Church that is in their house.

We have other people too.

> **1st Corinthians 16:**15 I beseech you, brethren, (ye know the house of Stephanas, that it is the firstfruits of Achaia, and that they have addicted themselves to

the ministry of the saints,)

This was a household addicted to ministry.

> **Romans 16:7** Salute Andronicus and Junia, my kinsmen, and my fellowprisoners, who are of note among the apostles, who also were in Christ before me.

This was arguably a couple and also were apostles.

> **Romans 16:15** Salute Philologus, and Julia, Nereus, and his sister, and Olympas, and all the saints which are with them.

These were siblings heading a local Church ministry.

We can go on and on. Siblings, married couples did lead Churches. Therefore, it is not forbidden in Scriptures.

In fact, Paul alluded to a generational influence In Timothy's ministry.

> **2ⁿᵈ Timothy 1:5** When I call to remembrance the unfeigned faith that is in thee, which dwelt first in thy grandmother Lois, and thy mother Eunice; and I am persuaded that in thee also.

Never forgetting, it is not so in every instance, at least, not Peter or even Paul's family. Yet, it must not be frowned at as unscriptural if families, couples, siblings lead ministries.

Rather than get sentimental like saying "is it now family business etc.?" Let us ask the right questions.

- Are they capable according to Scriptures cited earlier?
- Can we see grace in them?

Or

- Did they become unqualified simply because they are family related?

I recall engaging a colleague who kept ranting about how some Churches had children who succeeded their parents as leaders in ministry. I let him finish and laughed at his hypocrisy since he was a Methodist. This was a Church founded and led and succeeded by siblings, Charles and John Wesley.

History is replete with great revivals led by relatives. This includes Churches too.

Yes, some were not as effective as others. This is the same as other instances where it was not led by family relations. Hence, it was not the family ties that "killed the ministry!"

If Aquila passed on to glory before Priscilla, you will not sue the ministry to court if Priscilla runs the Church as leader alone. This is the same with others earlier mentioned.

Only proven men are put in leadership.

If it happens that the predecessor led with family members, surely, it must be more reliable to hand over to faithful and tested men who might turn out to be his family.

We are to be very discreet in ordination.

1st Timothy 5:22 Lay hands suddenly on no man,

However, give responsibility to tested men.

2nd Timothy 2:2 And the things that thou hast heard of me among many witnesses, the same commit thou to faithful men, who shall be able to teach others also.

No one often suits this better than those who have worked with you more closely and you can trust.

Philippians 2:19 But I trust in the Lord Jesus to send Timotheus shortly unto you, that I also may be of good comfort, when I know your state. **Vs 20** For I have no man likeminded, who will naturally care for your state. **Vs 21** For all seek their own, not the things which are Jesus Christ's. **Vs 22** But ye know the proof of him, that, as a son with the father, he hath served with me in the gospel.

Paul's words here are personal. It was about how Timothy served Paul.

It happens that some are family related. We should not throw fits over that if it happens.

I do not know any sane person who will not want his household with him in ministry, faithfully serving and able to succeed you in ministry.

In my own opinion, Joshua flaunted this.

> **Joshua 24:15** And if it seem evil unto you to serve the Lord , choose you this day whom ye will serve; whether the gods which your fathers served that were on the other side of the flood, or the gods of the Amorites, in whose land ye dwell: but as for me and my house, we will serve the Lord .

Therefore, rather than get into unnecessary debates over this, pray and work to see your own family serve God with you in ministry.

What glory it would be to His name if this should be for us all.

Questions and answers on women in ministry

Q- Does Scriptures allow Women lead men in the Churches?

A- why do you ask; which Scriptures suggest otherwise?

Q – **1ˢᵗ Corinthians 14:34-35** Let your women keep silence in the Churches: for it is not permitted unto them to speak; but they are commanded to be under obedience, as also saith the law.
Vs 35 And if they will learn any thing, let them ask their husbands at home: for it is a shame for women to speak in the Church.

Seem to say so

A- if you consider well ALL such texts on women and men and submission, they are all marital instructions not concerning leadership in Church;

Ephesians 5:22 Wives, submit yourselves unto your own husbands, as unto the Lord.

Colossians 3:18 Wives, submit yourselves unto your own husbands, as it is fit in the Lord.

1st Timothy 2:11-15 Let the woman learn in silence with all subjection. **Vs 12** But I suffer not a woman to teach, nor to usurp authority over the man, but to be in silence. **Vs 13** For Adam was first formed, then Eve. **Vs 14** And Adam was not deceived, but the woman being deceived was in the transgression. **Vs 15** Notwithstanding she shall be saved in childbearing, if they continue in faith and charity and holiness with sobriety.

1st Peter 3:5 For after this manner in the old time the holy women also, who trusted in God, adorned themselves, being in subjection unto their own husbands:

1st Corinthians 11:3 But I would have you know, that the head of every man is Christ; and the head of the woman is the man; and the head of Christ is God.

Hope this is Clear?

Q- what then could the 1 Corinthians 14:35 imply?

A- exactly what I stated earlier, Let me add, if this is given a blanket application even at Corinth then we would have a place of deep confusion!

For example,

Women would only be allowed to prophesy to women

1st Corinthians 11:5 But every woman that prayeth or prophesieth with her head uncovered dishonoureth her head: for that is even all one as if she were shaven.

1st Corinthians 14:31 For ye may all prophesy one by one, that all may learn, and all may be comforted.

It would mean women can not participate in believers meetings too;

1st Corinthians 14:26 How is it then, brethren? when ye come together, every one of you hath a psalm, hath a doctrine, hath a tongue, hath a revelation, hath an interpretation. Let all things be done unto edifying.

Doctrine means instruction.

It will be impossible for women to lead praise in Church too, since it involves teaching and admonition

Colossians 3:16 Let the word of Christ dwell in you richly in all wisdom; teaching and admonishing one another in psalms and hymns and spiritual songs, singing with grace in your hearts to the Lord.

Except if it means, women would only sing to women.

Not even leading prayer is possible.

Women can't even undertake the great commission;

Matthew 28:19-20 Go ye therefore, and teach all nations, baptizing them in the name of the Father, and of the Son, and of the Holy Ghost: **Vs 20** Teaching them to observe all things whatsoever I have commanded you: and, lo, I am with you alway, even unto the end of the world. Amen.

This is discipleship except if only to women, it further implies a woman can't evangelize male unbelievers

Q- But why did Jesus not include women amongst his apostles

A- That is not of much importance here, he had others who accompanied him in ministry who were women, more so the woman at the well in John preached Christ

John 4:28 The woman then left her waterpot, and went her way into the city, and saith to the men, **Vs 29** Come, see a man, which told me all things that ever I did: is not this the Christ? **Vs 30** Then they went out of the city, and came unto him...**Vs 39** And many of the Samaritans of that city believed on him for the saying of the woman, which testified, He told me all that ever I did.

It is a fact that all his apostles were also all Jewish even though ministry work wasn't restricted to Jews.

Q- Paul also included being a husband of one wife as

qualification for Church leadership, which automatically disqualifies women

A- Not so, if you checked those qualifications in 1 Timothy 3 (which is implied here) Paul would be disqualified on two counts as well

> **1 Timothy 3:2** A bishop then must be blameless, the husband of one wife, vigilant, sober, of good behaviour, given to hospitality, apt to teach; **Vs 4** One that ruleth well his own house, having his children in subjection with all gravity; **Vs 5** (For if a man know not how to rule his own house, how shall he take care of the Church of God?)

Also, the Pauline epistles have examples of women in leadership.

For example, **Priscilla**

> **Romans 16:3** Greet Priscilla and Aquila my helpers in Christ Jesus: **Vs 4** Who have for my life laid down their own necks: unto whom not only I give thanks, but also all the Churches of the Gentiles. **Vs 5** Likewise greet the Church that is in their house. Salute my wellbeloved Epaenetus, who is the firstfruits of Achaia unto Christ.

> **1st Corinthians 16:19** The Churches of Asia salute you. Aquila and Priscilla salute you much in the

Lord, with the Church that is in their house.

Luke records her as a teacher.

> **Acts 18:26** And he began to speak boldly in the synagogue: whom when Aquila and Priscilla had heard, they took him unto them, and expounded unto him the way of God more perfectly.

The pronouns and prepositions show her as very active alongside her husband.

Also, arguably she functioned like an apostle

There was also **Junia**

> **Romans 16:7** Salute Andronicus and Junia, my kinsmen, and my fellowprisoners, who are of note among the apostles, who also were in Christ before me.

This has been debated by many but it's more of being disagreeable.

Q- Obviously, women didn't feature prominently leadership then.

A- It had nothing to do with God but men

In the events surrounding the birth of Christ etc. women featured much

Luke 1:41-45 And it came to pass, that, when Elisabeth heard the salutation of Mary, the babe leaped in her womb; and Elisabeth was filled with the Holy Ghost: **Vs 42** And she spake out with a loud voice, and said, Blessed art thou among women, and blessed is the fruit of thy womb. **Vs 43** And whence is this to me, that the mother of my Lord should come to me? **Vs 44** For, lo, as soon as the voice of thy salutation sounded in mine ears, the babe leaped in my womb for joy. **Vs 45** And blessed is she that believed: for there shall be a performance of those things which were told her from the Lord.

She prophesied.

Luke 2:36-38 And there was one Anna, a prophetess, the daughter of Phanuel, of the tribe of Aser: she was of a great age, and had lived with an husband seven years from her virginity; **Vs 37** And she was a widow of about fourscore and four years, which departed not from the temple, but served God with fastings and prayers night and day. **Vs 38** And she coming in that instant gave thanks likewise unto the Lord, and spake of him to all them that looked for redemption in Jerusalem.

I had cited the woman in **John 4** earlier

Luke 8:2-3 And certain women, which had been

healed of evil spirits and infirmities, Mary called Magdalene, out of whom went seven devils, **Vs 3** And Joanna the wife of Chuza Herod's steward, and Susanna, and many others, which ministered unto him of their substance.

Some others featured prominently too in no small way

Very vitally is a crucial detail in His redemptive work

> **John 20:17-18** Jesus saith unto her, Touch me not; for I am not yet ascended to my Father: but go to my brethren, and say unto them, I ascend unto my Father, and your Father; and to my God, and your God. **Vs 18** Mary Magdalene came and told the disciples that she had seen the Lord, and that he had spoken these things unto her.

This was the very first witness of His resurrection, who disclosed to us the very vital truth of His ascension to the Father

Furthermore, Peter's first sermon could not have precluded women in the things and ministry of the spirit

> **Acts 2:17** And it shall come to pass in the last days, saith God, I will pour out of my Spirit upon all flesh: and your sons and your daughters shall prophesy, and your young men shall see visions, and your old

men shall dream dreams: **Vs 18** And on my servants and on my handmaidens I will pour out in those days of my Spirit; and they shall prophesy:

Q- So won't the earlier instructions to the married women affect a woman in leadership if her husband is in the Church?

A- No, if the husband is spiritual, he should know his domestic authority never extends to the Church.

I suppose many pastors really need to fully teach the New Testament and who we are in Christ, this is the only cure for our patriarchal psychology.

Q- But the **1st Timothy 3** still leaves a bit of unclear ends

A- not really

Though I left it like that and I usually do till much later but either way it should make us think.

Questions and answers about "full time ministry"

Q- What is full time ministry?

A- It is not a word in the epistles, it is likely a carryover from the Old Testament about the Levites, who stayed away from work secular majorly and were taken care of by other tribes.

Q- Is it wrong for a minister to work secular whilst being a pastor?

A- To the contrary, Scriptures support ministers to work for a living...

> **Acts 18:3** And because he was of the same craft, he abode with them, and wrought: for by their occupation they were tentmakers.

Paul, Priscilla and Aquila, were referred to here.

Acts 20:34 Yea, ye yourselves know, that these hands have ministered unto my necessities, and to them that were with me.

1st Thessalonians 2:9 For ye remember, brethren, our labour and travail: for labouring night and day, because we would not be chargeable unto any of you, we preached unto you the gospel of God.

"We" here refers to Paul, Silas and other apostles.

Q- Isn't this because the ministry was still young, that's why Paul had to work to support himself

A- That's not true, the Scriptures I just gave you refer to Paul after over 15-20 years in ministry

Let me give more instances

1st Corinthians 4:12 And labour, working with our own hands: being reviled, we bless; being persecuted, we suffer it:

1st Corinthians 9:6 Or I only and Barnabas, have not we power to forbear working?

2nd Thessalonians 3:8 Neither did we eat any man's bread for nought; but wrought with labour and travail night and day, that we might not be chargeable to any of you:

These Churches were very large in those days. Obviously, Paul and his associates did not work secularly because of these reasons you gave but rather to be exemplary and avoid greed and also to ensure the gospel was not /is not corrupted

Q- Was Paul a full-time minister

A- in our modern terms, no, but in biblical terms yes.

He never shirked in his duties

> **1st Corinthians 15:10** But by the grace of God I am what I am: and his grace which was bestowed upon me was not in vain; but I laboured more abundantly than they all: yet not I, but the grace of God which was with me.

He was laboring in his career and in ministry.

Q- Is it wrong for anyone to Abandon his career and go into ministry

A- No it is not, but he would not have a New Testament text to fully support this

Q- What about the text that " those who preach the gospel should live by the gospel

A- That is quoting Paul out of context

1ˢᵗ Corinthians 9:11 If we have sown unto you spiritual things, is it a great thing if we shall reap your carnal things? **Vs 12** If others be partakers of this power over you, are not we rather? Nevertheless, we have not used this power; but suffer all things, lest we should hinder the gospel of Christ. **Vs 13** Do ye not know that they which minister about holy things live of the things of the temple? and they which wait at the altar are partakers with the altar? **Vs 14** Even so hath the Lord ordained that they which preach the gospel should live of the gospel.

He was referring to supporting preachers not ministers not doing secular work.

Q- But should we still support ministers who work secularly

A- of course, what we give our teachers is honour not for welfare

Galatians 6:6 Let him that is taught in the word communicate unto him that teacheth in all good things.

1ˢᵗ Timothy 5:17 Let the elders that rule well be counted worthy of double honour, especially they who labour in the word and doctrine. **Vs 18** For the Scripture saith, thou shalt not muzzle the ox that treadeth out the corn. And, the labourer is worthy of his reward.

Nothing stops us from giving and doing it very well. It is out of respect and in response to their labours.

Q-But what about the disciples of Jesus, they abandoned their professions to follow him

A- Scriptures please?

Q- **Luke 5:11** And when they had brought their ships to land, they forsook all, and followed him.

> **Mark 10:28** Then Peter began to say unto him, Lo, we have left all, and have followed thee.

A- We must not deduct finalities here

For example, the **Mark 10:28** example should help

> **Mark 10:29** And Jesus answered and said, Verily I say unto you, there is no man that hath left house, or brethren, or sisters, or father, or mother, or wife, or children, or lands, for my sake, and the gospel's,

The issue here is language, the "forsaking" must be seen as prioritizing. Am sure you know they did not "renounce" their families.

In fact, latter texts support this

> **John 21:3** Simon Peter saith unto them, I go a fishing. They say unto him; we also go with thee. They went forth, and entered into a ship immediately; and that night they caught nothing.

They still had ships, nets etc.

Some assume they back slid here, I used to too But that is deducing meaning where there is no such opinion available.

Truth is Paul and his associates always found how to use their skills to earn money in their missionary journeys.
Like a mobile business man

Q- But won't working secular hinder the work of ministry

A- Paul wrote over half of the New Testament books, the issue is many of us just have a mindset that should be renewed.

Q- If you would advise a young minister on this what would you tell him

A- Get a job, business venture etc. ensure it allows you to function effectively. It does not hinder prayer, pastoring, teaching or Church work. Rather it helps cure greed, covetousness and using the gospel as a means for gain

Paul warned Timothy on this

> **1 Timothy 6:5** Perverse disputings of men of corrupt minds, and destitute of the truth, supposing that gain is godliness: from such withdraw thyself. **Vs 6** But godliness with contentment is great gain.

As an example, the local Church where I serve as pastor operates this model.

I think we study, pray, teach, minister and reach the world by God's grace.

We only need to be committed to the work and never put money and our welfare above the work and nothing shall by any means hurt you.

A lesson I learnt during the last holidays

I draw lessons a lot via observation.

During the last festive season I observed a couple of instructive things, some of which I shared during our last workers meeting in the Church I serve as Pastor.

I had cause to visit airports and noticed it was busy and active because those who managed it were not on holidays or in a festive mood, in fact the security men were at utmost diligence.

Also, I observed Doctors and health workers had to be at their beats, they had no luxury of jollification whilst all others were in such mood.

Festive season or not, men will fall ill and need attention, else more disaster could overwhelm all the fun and excitement.

Same for traffic control, they were not found in parties (most) or else many of us will experience untold traffic and avoidable terror on the roads.

Electricity too was served, simply because those in charge had to suspend holidays so we all could afford some fun and enjoy services.

Even entertainers were busy in so much that they weren't offering more than the required fun for such a festive period, same with footballers.

Then like the Teacher in Ecclesiastes;

It came to my understanding that some duties require full concentration.

Those that are referred to as essential duties are so called because they require 24 hours input, alertness and dedication. Security, Health etc.

How much more the Preacher of the gospel; the pastor or Christian leader.

Such ministry is far more essential than those highlighted above. Men's eternities depend on them.

Satan does not holiday, neither does sin, sickness and oppression.

We must be found at our duty posts. Even when as it were we must do earthly things we must not lose our edge, be found frivolous and not be sensitive.

In one of Jesus' parables he pointed out a fact when men are off beat and even asleep

Matthew 13:25 But while men slept, his enemy came and sowed tares among the wheat, and went his way.

Prayer, Meditation, study etc. must be diligently observed even when off the pulpit and doing other things.

As Paul told Timothy

2nd Timothy 2:4 No man that warreth entangleth himself with the affairs of this life; that he may please him who hath chosen him to be a soldier.

Our job demands full time concentration. In season and out of season

2nd Timothy 4:2 Preach the word; be instant in season, out of season;

You must be at your duty post at all times else there will be untold commotion and avoidable challenges

DOCTRINAL MATTERS

What Bible teaching is not (1)

Bible teaching is the core reason for Christian fellowship. Jesus commands that we teach all nations as part of His work in the earth.

> **Matthew 28:19** Go ye therefore, and teach all nations, baptizing them in the name of the Father, and of the Son, and of the Holy Ghost: **Vs 20** Teaching them to observe all things whatsoever I have commanded you: and, lo, I am with you alway, *even* unto the end of the world. Amen.

He mentions teaching twice. Hence, this was the tradition of the apostles after His ascension.

> **Acts 2:42** And they continued stedfastly in the apostles' doctrine and fellowship, and in breaking of bread, and in prayers.

They taught from house to house and in public meetings too.

> **Acts 20:20** *And* how I kept back nothing that was profitable *unto you,* but have shewed you, and have taught you publickly, and from house to house,

A fundamental ingredient of leadership in the Church is

the grasp of doctrine.

> **1ˢᵗ Timothy 4:16** Take heed unto thyself, and unto the doctrine; continue in them: for in doing this thou shalt both save thyself, and them that hear thee.

Doctrine does not mean rules and regulations but teaching and explanation which can involve instructions.

> **1ˢᵗ Timothy 4:11** These things command and teach.

Anyone who cannot explain must not be put in leadership.

> **1ˢᵗ Timothy 3:2** A bishop … apt to teach;

That is, able to explain.

We must count such as worthy leaders.

> **1ˢᵗ Timothy 5:17** Let the elders that rule well be counted worthy of double honour, especially they who labour in the word and doctrine.

Teaching simply means to explain. It is done with the mental comprehension of the audience in mind. The minister must explain the Scriptures. He does this with the Scriptures.

A typical example can be found in Luke's account of Jesus.

> **Luke 24:27** And beginning at Moses and all the prophets, he expounded unto them in all the Scriptures the things concerning himself.

The word "beginning" is an original word for sequential arrangement. Teaching is orderly; no rush, no hurries, no haste. He took on ALL the pages of Scriptures.

He expounded. This means to give meanings; not your subjective meaning but the very objective meanings. Teaching is never mysterious. It is usually very clear.

> **Luke 24:32** And they said one to another, Did not our heart burn within us, while he talked with us by the way, and while he opened to us the Scriptures?

Their hearts could see it; it burned with clarity.

Later on, he taught again.

Teaching is gradual.

> **Luke 24:45** Then opened he their understanding, that they might understand the Scriptures

The term "understanding" (used twice) implies to put the facts together. Here, the teacher ensures no grey areas. He draws all the sides together. All texts are examined contextually and with full view of all the contents.

All mysteries ended at the advent of Christ and His giving of the Spirit.

> **Luke 8:10** And he said, Unto you it is given to know the mysteries of the kingdom of God

It is given to us to know.

> **John 16:13** Howbeit when he, the Spirit of truth, is come, he will guide you into all truth: for he shall not speak of himself; but whatsoever he shall hear, that shall he speak: and he will shew you things to come.

The Spirit will guide us into ALL truth.

Again, this is not a subjective "spirit" interpretation.

A background will let you know that he Spirit has so far ONLY communicated truths in written form.

> **1ˢᵗ Peter 1:10** Of which salvation the prophets have enquired and searched diligently, who prophesied of the grace that should come unto you: **Vs 11** Searching what, or what manner of time the Spirit of Christ which was in them did signify, when it

testified beforehand the sufferings of Christ, and the glory that should follow. **Vs 12** Unto whom it was revealed, that not unto themselves, but unto us they did minister the things, which are now reported unto you by them that have preached the gospel unto you with the Holy Ghost sent down from heaven; which things the angels desire to look into.

This refers to the Old Testament books of the Bible. The Prophets wrote them. The Spirit is accorded as the source.

Paul inferred this.

2nd Timothy 3:16 All Scripture is given by inspiration of God, and is profitable for doctrine, for reproof, for correction, for instruction in righteousness:

The Spirit reveals and instructs via the written form; word.

Thus, Jesus' promise in **John 16:13** has been fulfilled by the penning of the epistles.

1st Corinthians 2:12 Now we have received, not the spirit of the world, but the spirit which is of God; that we might know the things that are freely given to us of God. **Vs 13** Which things also we speak, not in the words which man's wisdom teacheth, but which the Holy Ghost teacheth; comparing spiritual things with spiritual.

Paul refers to his teaching the Church.

"We speak" refers to the apostles and the term "comparing spiritual" refers to the comprehension distinction of recipients of the Spirit for the Spirit's revelation has been written.

> **Ephesians 3:3** How that by revelation he made known unto me the mystery; (as I wrote afore in few words, **Vs 4** Whereby, when ye read, ye may understand my knowledge in the mystery of Christ) **Vs 5** Which in other ages was not made known unto the sons of men, as it is now revealed unto his holy apostles and prophets by the Spirit;

It was written to be read.

Peter acknowledged this too.

> **2nd Peter 3:15** And account that the longsuffering of our Lord is salvation; even as our beloved brother Paul also according to the wisdom given unto him hath written unto you; **Vs 16** As also in all his epistles, speaking in them of these things; in which are some things hard to be understood, which they

that are unlearned and unstable wrest, as they do also the other Scriptures, unto their own destruction.

Paul also instructed Timothy to teach the Scriptures.

> **2ⁿᵈ Timothy 3:17** That the man of God may be perfect, throughly furnished unto all good works.

Jesus taught the same way.

Bible teachers must teach the Bible; what is written. We do this via explanation.

Isaiah gave us a hint.

> **Isaiah 28:9** Whom shall he teach knowledge? and whom shall he make to understand doctrine? them that are weaned from the milk, and drawn from the breasts. **Vs 10** For precept must be upon precept, precept upon precept; line upon line, line upon line; here a little, and there a little:

Teaching means to explain in detail; no jumpstarts.

For example, you may think sons are the advanced stage of the new birth. An angel might even appear to you to tell you.

Galatians 1:8 But though we, or an angel from heaven, preach any other gospel unto you than that which we have preached unto you, let him be accursed.

However, if that is not what Paul wrote, then you are wrong.

Galatians 4:1 Now I say, That the heir, as long as he is a child, differeth nothing from a servant, though he be lord of all; **Vs 2** But is under tutors and governors until the time appointed of the father. **Vs 3** Even so we, when we were children, were in bondage under the elements of the world: **Vs 4** But when the fulness of the time was come, God sent forth his Son, made of a woman, made under the law,

Paul uses children and sons.

However, if you read it further and back up earlier, it becomes very clear.

He is referring to the same people. The sons are the children. A man's heir (which son implies here) is His child.

Again, the teacher must be patient and not rush to conclusion.

The use of revelation never implies discovering a hidden meaning. The words used are NOT heavenly or mysterious words. They are words with earthly meanings but may carry spiritual implications. Revelation here simply means revelation in the mind, not in the Scriptures.

The Scriptures are the revelation; they are revealed and written.

> **Ephesians 1:17** That the God of our Lord Jesus Christ, the Father of glory, may give unto you the spirit of wisdom and revelation in the knowledge of him: **Vs 18** The eyes of your understanding being enlightened; that ye may know what is the hope of his calling, and what the riches of the glory of his inheritance in the saints.

He prayed for revelation. This means that their minds are opened to what is written.

A further explanation will suffice.

> **Ephesians 3:4** Whereby, when ye read, ye may understand my knowledge in the mystery of Christ)

This prayer can only get answered when you READ, then you understand. Hence, the teacher must get us to read.

1ˢᵗ Timothy 4:13 Till I come, give attendance to reading, to exhortation, to doctrine.

We must have a grasp of details. Hence, when next you want to teach, ensure you explain. There should be no hidden meanings. Bible teaching is no esoteric information. It means the audience on its own can verify the facts you gave. This verification is done ONLY in the Scriptures.

Acts 17:11 These were more noble than those in Thessalonica, in that they received the word with all readiness of mind, and searched the Scriptures daily, whether those things were so.

They searched the Scriptures.

Just like Jesus taught,

Luke 24:44 And he said unto them, These are the words which I spake unto you, while I was yet with you, that all things must be fulfilled, which were written in the law of Moses, and in the prophets, and in the psalms, concerning me. **Vs 45** Then opened he their understanding, that they might understand the Scriptures,

A true teacher must teach from what is written; explain the context, pretext, post- text and all within the contents of Scriptures.

What Bible teaching is not (2)

The teaching of Scriptures is the definition of doctrine.

2ⁿᵈ Timothy 3:16 All Scripture is given by inspiration of God, and is profitable for doctrine, for reproof, for correction, for instruction in righteousness:

The Scriptures refer to what is written. It is a fact that these are words inscribed in the pages of the Bible; a book which explains itself. It should be read and understood.

Ephesians 3:3 How that by revelation he made known unto me the mystery; (as I wrote afore in few words, **Vs 4** Whereby, when ye read, ye may understand my knowledge in the mystery of Christ)

It was written to be read.

Jesus harped on this fact of reading.

Matthew 19:4 And he answered and said unto them, Have ye not read, that he which made them at the beginning made them male and female,

He said this severally.

The term "read" means to view, mentally capture and appraise words written. This implies that the teacher must read and have his audience read too.

1st Timothy 4:13 Till I come, give attendance to reading, to exhortation, to doctrine.

True Bible teaching is study. It is not waiting at the speakers' table or stable for mind numbing, high sounding words called "revs". It is reasoning with the Scriptures which produce understanding.

Bible teaching / teachers must avoid playing to the gallery; using mere oratory to wow the listener.

1st Corinthians 2:1 And I, brethren, when I came to you, came not with excellency of speech or of wisdom, declaring unto you the testimony of God… **Vs 4** And my speech and my preaching was not with enticing words of man's wisdom, but in demonstration of the Spirit and of power:

Scriptures MUST be well explained in very clear and painstaking fashion, not a noise making, soap box theatrics dilly dallying. Bible teaching is no circus show or magical arts. This is often applied by heretics who quickly point to results and self - testimonies.

Romans 16:18 For they that are such serve not our Lord Jesus Christ, but their own belly; and by good words and fair speeches deceive the hearts of the simple.

It is important we must not get in the way of people's understanding by feeding our audience a "testimony diet". We must stick to what and who the Scriptures reveal- Christ!

Romans 16:25 Now to him that is of power to stablish you according to my gospel, and the preaching of Jesus Christ, according to the revelation of the mystery, which was kept secret since the world began,

It is already laid and founded.

1st Corinthians 3:11 For other foundation can no man lay than that is laid, which is Jesus Christ.

Hence, he warns in **verse 10** that all must take heed to build upon it.

1st Corinthians 3:10 According to the grace of God which is given unto me, as a wise masterbuilder, I have laid the foundation, and another buildeth thereon. But let every man take heed how he buildeth thereupon.

Matthew 24:24 For there shall arise false Christs, and false prophets, and shall shew great signs and wonders; insomuch that, if it were possible, they shall deceive the very elect.

Signs and wonders accompany the gospel when preached but do not produce understanding of the message. The teacher must appeal to the understanding, and not the emotions of his listeners. Hence, the ability of the teacher to refute and present an unassailable explanation.

> **Titus 1:9** Holding fast the faithful word as he hath been taught, that he may be able by sound doctrine both to exhort and to convince the gainsayers.

He is able to convince.

Paul did this in Ephesus.

> **Acts 19:8** And he went into the synagogue, and spake boldly for the space of three months, disputing and persuading the things concerning the kingdom of God. **Vs 9** But when divers were hardened, and believed not, but spake evil of that way before the multitude, he departed from them, and separated the disciples, disputing daily in the school of one Tyrannus.

The teacher, just like Jesus did in the four gospels, is making convincing discussions by the way of clear reasoning and explanation, no esoteric acclamations.

Apollos presents a picture of this too.

> **Acts 18:24** And a certain Jew named Apollos, born at Alexandria, an eloquent man, and mighty in the Scriptures, came to Ephesus. **Vs 25** This man was instructed in the way of the Lord; and being fervent in the spirit, he spake and taught diligently the things of the Lord, knowing only the baptism of John.

The first and vital ingredient is a grasp of Scriptures. He must copiously quote the Scriptures and be diligent in explanation.

Another key element we shall see is the ability to receive more information.

Note that Apollos knew ONLY John's baptism even though his message was Christ.

Teaching ministries grow.

> **Acts 18:26** And he began to speak boldly in the synagogue: whom when Aquila and Priscilla had heard, they took him unto them , and expounded unto him the way of God more perfectly. They explained more to him.He kept learning… **Vs 28** For he mightily convinced the Jews, and that publickly, shewing by the Scriptures that Jesus was Christ.

His explanation improved but his tool remained Scriptures not foreign materials.

The ministry must only be founded upon the written word.

Apollos later became a renowned teacher.

1st Corinthians 3:6 I have planted, Apollos watered; but God gave the increase.

He is able to transmit information appropriately via adequate explanation. Remember, no grey areas. The teacher's aim is to produce maturity.

Colossians 1:28 Whom we preach, warning every man, and teaching every man in all wisdom; that we may present every man perfect in Christ Jesus:

His message must never lose its focus. It must never shift to the speaker but the Word, Christ Jesus.

2nd Corinthians 4:5 For we preach not ourselves, but Christ Jesus the Lord; and ourselves your servants for Jesus' sake.

Not us but Him; not my story but His story alone.

The meal for spiritual development must remain Christ.

Ephesians 4:13 Till we all come in the unity of the faith, and of the knowledge of the Son of God, unto a perfect man, unto the measure of the stature of the fulness of Christ: **Vs 14** That we henceforth be no more children, tossed to and fro, and carried about with every wind of doctrine, by the sleight of men, and cunning craftiness, whereby they lie in wait to deceive;

Bible teaching is not storytelling or testimony proclamations. It is explaining and reasoning the Scriptures to behold Christ. The speaker must be faithful with this.

> **1st Corinthians 4:1** Let a man so account of us, as of the ministers of Christ, and stewards of the mysteries of God. **Vs 2** Moreover it is required in stewards, that a man be found faithful.

He must understand he holds the mystery of God unveiled.

Faithfulness here implies consistency. He must never change his focus because of his audience cravings.

> **2nd Timothy 4:3** For the time will come when they will not endure sound doctrine; but after their own lusts shall they heap to themselves teachers, having itching ears;

He must be faithful to the message.

Paul recognizes this in his instruction to Timothy.

2nd Timothy 2:2 And the things that thou hast heard of me among many witnesses, the same commit thou to faithful men, who shall be able to teach others also.

The same.

If we only followed the instructions of the apostles, our explanations of Christ may differ in depth but never in information.

We will not have the cacophony of voices abounding today called "personal revs". Scriptures authorize no individual to have a unique or personal revelation.

He might understand in levels but must never see Scriptures away from what is written.

What Bible teaching is not (3)

Scriptures are written for reading and learning.

Romans 15:4 For whatsoever things were written aforetime were written for our learning, that we through patience and comfort of the Scriptures might have hope.

We must read to understand.

Ephesians 3:4 Whereby, when ye read, ye may understand my knowledge in the mystery of Christ)

The teacher must do the same.

We have since seen Scriptures used as a mere reference; where we quote. We formed this habit simply because it has been chaptalized and versed. However, this was only done in the 13th and 16th centuries respectively. The original letters were never put in chapters and verses. This implies that the writers intended we read the WHOLE piece together. Hence, the speakers of

Scriptures referenced the entire books in speaking of portions of it.

> **Galatians 3:8** And the Scripture, foreseeing that God would justify the heathen through faith, preached before the gospel unto Abraham, saying , In thee shall all nations be blessed.

To know which Scripture he is speaking about, you will need to read the entire book of Genesis and locate the life of Abraham there. You will need to read through the ENTIRE book to pick out that text, which by the way today is made easier with verses and chapters. Back then, you are very unlikely to quote this out of context as you must have read through the whole book!

> **Galatians 4:21** Tell me, ye that desire to be under the law, do ye not hear the law? **Vs 22** For it is written, that Abraham had two sons, the one by a bondmaid, the other by a freewoman.

Same here.

Hence, when the apostles taught, the listeners had to consult the materials themselves and read through as well.

> **Acts 17:11** These were more noble than those in Thessalonica, in that they received the word with all readiness of mind, and searched the Scriptures daily,

whether those things were so.

Hence, a teacher of the Bible is one who knows THE SCRIPTURES!

2nd Timothy 3:15 And that from a child thou hast known the holy Scriptures, which are able to make thee wise unto salvation through faith which is in Christ Jesus. **Vs 16** All Scripture is given by inspiration of God, and is profitable for doctrine, for reproof, for correction, for instruction in righteousness:

It is "All Scriptures" not the "faith message" or "radical grace" or "holiness" or "prosperity message". The Bible teacher MUST apply basic rules of reading and explaining literary materials. He must not speak like a "genie" or "magician". He must not treat Scriptures like a book of esoteric words. Furthermore, he must read the texts together.

Just like Jesus did,

Luke 24:27 And beginning at Moses and all the prophets, he expounded unto them in all the Scriptures the things concerning himself. **Vs 44** And he said unto them, These are the words which I spake unto you, while I was yet with you, that all things must be fulfilled, which were written in the law of Moses, and in the prophets, and in the psalms, concerning me. **Vs 45** Then opened he their understanding, that they might understand the Scriptures,

When he does this he will not lift verses / texts out of contexts. He will depart from an emergent style that I refer to as "concordance preaching". I have nothing against the use of concordances to study personally, though, I hardly use them. Words may have the same meanings generally but applications will usually differ in context. Many errors have emerged from studying and teaching this way.

Many have become lazy with the advent of apps and easy ways of studying. You must read through and teach contextually. Pretext refers to earlier verses while post text refers to later verses. Hence, you read the pretext, the post text and bring ALL within context.

Let me cite a few (though I have hundreds up my mind right now!):

> **Hebrews 11:1** Now faith is the substance of things hoped for, the evidence of things not seen.

We have heard many try to define faith this way.

However, the Bible is no dictionary of definitions. It is a story, the story of Christ's (God) descent into man's sin and his descent eventually into man himself.

Jesus said this much.

> **John 5:39** Search the Scriptures; for in them ye think ye have eternal life: and they are they which testify of me. **Vs 40** And ye will not come to me, that ye might have life.

Let us get back to the earlier text.

I have heard some preach, "faith is NOW, if it is not "now", it is not faith. This is not bad, but using this text in **Hebrews 11** as a definition of faith is awful study.

The term "now" means therefore, that is,"based on this ".

Based on what?

> **Hebrews 10:36** For ye have need of patience, that, after ye have done the will of God, ye might receive the promise. **Vs 37** For yet a little while, and he that shall come will come, and will not tarry. **Vs 38** Now the just shall live by faith: but if any man draw back, my soul shall have no pleasure in him. **Vs 39** But we are not of them who draw back unto perdition; but of them that believe to the saving of the soul.

Who are the "them"?

The terms "we" and "them" are two different expressions of reference.

Obviously, this text refers to an expectation of "he that shall come". It is a faith expecting a person.

It is important to note that this text was quoted from **Habakkuk 2:3-4**.

> **Habakkuk 2:3** For the vision is yet for an appointed time, but at the end it shall speak, and not lie: though it tarry, wait for it; because it will surely come, it will not tarry. **Vs 4** Behold, his soul which is lifted up is not upright in him: but the just shall live by his faith.

Obviously, it is a prophecy. Hence, the book of Hebrews explains this and its fulfillment.

Observe the Post text.

> **Hebrews 11:2** For by it the elders obtained a good report. **Vs 3** Through faith we understand that the worlds were framed by the word of God, so that things which are seen were not made of things which do appear.

The elders were the "them" that did not draw back but believed to be saved. They obtained a good report. From Abel to the last person, their faith hoped for and expected things they had not seen. Their faith waited. This is not faith today!

Hence the post texts,

Hebrews 11:13 These all died in faith, not having received the promises, but having seen them afar off, and were persuaded of them , and embraced them , and confessed that they were strangers and pilgrims on the earth… **Vs 39** And these all, having obtained a good report through faith, received not the promise: **Vs 40** God having provided some better thing for us, that they without us should not be made perfect.

They looked forward.

Hence, the next verse says that we look away from them, that is, from the Old Testament examples since Christ has fulfilled their expectation.

Hebrews 12:1 Wherefore seeing we also are compassed about with so great a cloud of witnesses, let us lay aside every weight, and the sin which doth so easily beset us , and let us run with patience the race that is set before us,

They had a good report of expectation waiting for Christ. He is the substance of the things and evidence of the things.

Hebrews 12:2 Looking unto Jesus the author and finisher of our faith; who for the joy that was set before him endured the cross, despising the shame, and is set down at the right hand of the throne of God.

We look unto Jesus, who authored (began) the faith by speaking to them (**Hebrews 11:3**) in promises and perfected it by his death, resurrection and ascension which fulfills their expectation.

Hence, today, just like and with us, they have come to fulfillment.

> **Hebrews 12:22** But ye are come unto mount Sion, and unto the city of the living God, the heavenly Jerusalem, and to an innumerable company of angels, **Vs 23** To the general assembly and Church of the firstborn, which are written in heaven, and to God the Judge of all, and to the spirits of just men made perfect,

Spirits are now made perfect. Reading the earlier parts of the book shows that they without us were not made perfect.

The term "prefect" refers to the effect of Jesus' sacrifice.

> **Hebrews 10:14** For by one offering he hath perfected for ever them that are sanctified.

Without his blood offered, no one was made perfect. Hence, His being called "perfecter of faith" refers not to us but them. He accomplished their expectation.

Hence, his reference to Abel's blood which cannot be his blood but rather the blood of his animal offering. This is so simple if read in context.

> **Hebrews 11:4** By faith Abel offered unto God a more excellent sacrifice than Cain, by which he obtained witness that he was righteous, God testifying of his gifts: and by it he being dead yet speaketh.

It simply means Abel's animal blood offering was in expectation, that is, the substance of things hoped for, which is Christ's death hoped for.

Earlier, the writer simplified the tithing practice. Many have assumed he was teaching to tithe but that is very preposterous.

> **Hebrews 7:5** And verily they that are of the sons of Levi, who receive the office of the priesthood, have a commandment to take tithes of the people according to the law, that is, of their brethren, though they come out of the loins of Abraham: **Vs 6** But he whose descent is not counted from them received tithes of Abraham, and blessed him that had the promises. **Vs 7** And without all contradiction the less is blessed of the better. **Vs 8** And here men that die receive tithes; but there he receiveth them , of whom it is witnessed that he liveth. **Vs 9** And as I may so say, Levi also, who receiveth tithes, payed tithes in Abraham. **Vs 10** For he was yet in the loins of his

father, when Melchisedec met him.

It indicates honour and says that Melchizedek is greater than Levi. That is the reason for the entire historical parody. He makes it clearer why Moses' law did not achieve much when he simply added the golden fact, that in Levi, all (Jews) paid tithes in Abraham!

 Some claim Jesus takes tithes! That is ridiculous. It is a deliberate misreading of verse 8,

> **Hebrews 7:8** And here men that die receive tithes; but there he receiveth them , of whom it is witnessed that he liveth.

The term "received them" is italicized. More so, he was referring to Melchizedek not Jesus and Melchizedek is not Jesus.

> **Hebrews 7:3** Without father, without mother, without descent, having neither beginning of days, nor end of life; but made like unto the Son of God; abideth a priest continually.

"Made like unto Jesus" indicates that he is a symbol. Therefore, just like all figurative narratives of the Old Testament, if we are honest and sincere, verses 9 &10 ought to end the tithing conundrum.

However, just like the love of money, anywhere this issue is discussed, its adherents act like jazzed men!

They will spew testimonies like heretics do to support extra biblical things. That said.

The teacher must not use Scripture texts for mere references. He must seek to make his audience comprehend the intended and objective meaning of texts. If he were a typical "proof texting concordance" teacher, he would have successfully used the above scenario to tell believers to tithe, whilst he simply pulled wool over their eyes.

This is the same with many other subjects.

For example,

> **Hebrews 12:14** Follow peace with all men, and holiness, without which no man shall see the Lord:

Using this text to ask men to be holy in order to make heaven is poor study.

The same writer discussed holiness in the entire book, which by the way is sanctification. He even used it for animals and vessels of the temple.

"Holy" simply means to take something for your exclusive use or ownership or pleasure.

> **Hebrews 2:11** For both he that sanctifieth and they who are sanctified are all of one: for which cause he is not ashamed to call them brethren,

Hebrews 3:1 Wherefore, holy brethren, partakers of the heavenly calling, consider the Apostle and High Priest of our profession, Christ Jesus;

Hebrews 10:10 By the which will we are sanctified through the offering of the body of Jesus Christ once for all.

Hence, how will he ask you to be holy after explaining Christ's work as making us holy! The man who has believed in Christ has seen the Lord by being made holy.

Hebrews 10:19 Having therefore, brethren, boldness to enter into the holiest by the blood of Jesus, **Vs 20** By a new and living way, which he hath consecrated for us, through the veil, that is to say, his flesh;

The teacher must never use Scriptures to back up his claims! He must be explaining Scriptures which have its own already written claims.

What Bible teaching is not (conclusion)

Bible teaching is the major reason for Christian gathering. It is the fulcrum for true Christian worship.

> **1st Timothy 3:15** But if I tarry long, that thou mayest know how thou oughtest to behave thyself in the house of God, which is the Church of the living God, the pillar and ground of the truth.

The term "pillar and ground of truth" implies where truth is disseminated. We ought to sing and pray when we gather and also minister to people's needs too but in order of priority, Bible teaching takes preeminence.

> **1st Timothy 4:13** Till I come, give attendance to reading, to exhortation, to doctrine.

Church services were designed by the Lord to be Bible study meetings. The "Great commission" implies teaching as a core practice.

Matthew 28:19 Go ye therefore, and teach all nations... **Vs 20** Teaching them...

Teaching is given emphasis.

The local Church ought to be breeding teachers more than any other type of worker.

2nd Timothy 2:2 And the things that thou hast heard of me among many witnesses, the same commit thou to faithful men, who shall be able to teach others also.

This was practiced much in,

Acts 11:26 And when he had found him, he brought him unto Antioch. And it came to pass, that a whole year they assembled themselves with the Church, and taught much people. And the disciples were called Christians first in Antioch.

A key ingredient of Bible teaching is the fact that the teacher learns what he teaches.

 I will re-emphasize an earlier quoted text.

2nd Timothy 2:2 And the things that thou hast heard of me among many witnesses, the same commit thou to faithful men, who shall be able to teach others also.

He emphasizes "the same things" and the fact that "you

heard of me" NOT from the "Spirit ".

> **2nd Timothy 3:14** But continue thou in the things which thou hast learned and hast been assured of, knowing of whom thou hast learned them;

He learns of another. He is taught and being taught. If an apostle like Timothy yet needed Paul to keep teaching him, then it is not right to assume a higher status.

He said the same to Titus.

> **Titus 1:9** Holding fast the faithful word as he hath been taught, that he may be able by sound doctrine both to exhort and to convince the gainsayers.

Note the statement "as he had been taught". Hence, there must be a semblance of doctrine and emphasis even though personalities may differ but the message is the same.

> **Ephesians 4:4** There is one body, and one Spirit, even as ye are called in one hope of your calling; **Vs 5** One Lord, one faith, one baptism, **Vs 6** One God and Father of all, who is above all, and through all, and in you all... **Vs 13** Till we all come in the unity of the faith, and of the knowledge of the Son of God, unto a perfect man, unto the measure of the stature of the fulness of Christ:

The message is the same as the Son of God.

He must remain a student, an ardent listener, a copious reader. He cannot but learn, for a good teacher is a good learner. Bible teaching is no personal empire of knowledge. It is not your fiefdom or kingdom of insights. The knowledge is not personal. It is a collective truth.

Furthermore, he cannot claim to have arrived at any juncture.

Hear Paul after 30 years in ministry.

> **Philippians 3:10** That I may know him, and the power of his resurrection, and the fellowship of his sufferings, being made conformable unto his death;

Even Peter recognized things he was getting to understand.

> **2nd Peter 3:16** As also in all his epistles, speaking in them of these things; in which are some things hard to be understood, which they that are unlearned and unstable wrest, as they do also the other Scriptures, unto their own destruction.

This is Peter's last epistle written towards his decease yet he makes this claim.

Hence, the teacher must keep learning!

Another ingredient in teaching is diligence. Bible

teaching cannot be whimsical. It cannot be handled by lazy men. It is not a soap box work.

> **Romans 16:18** For they that are such serve not our Lord Jesus Christ, but their own belly; and by good words and fair speeches deceive the hearts of the simple.

It deals with painstaking explanation of Scriptures. Bible teaching takes a duration of work. It involves labour.

> **2ⁿᵈ Timothy 2:15** Study to shew thyself approved unto God, a workman that needeth not to be ashamed, rightly dividing the word of truth.

The term "study" means labour, vigorous efforts and intense work. Rightly dividing refers to teaching.

> **2ⁿᵈ Timothy 2:24** And the servant of the Lord must not strive; but be gentle unto all men, apt to teach, patient,

He must be ready to teach for as long as it takes. When I see some Church services and the amount of time apportioned to sermons, I seriously doubt if they teach in there.

Jesus taught for hours.

> **Matthew 5:2** And he opened his mouth, and taught

them, saying,

Same with the apostles.

> **Acts 18:4** And he reasoned in the synagogue every sabbath, and persuaded the Jews and the Greeks.

This is every week.

> **Acts 18:25** This man was instructed in the way of the Lord; and being fervent in the spirit, he spake and taught diligently the things of the Lord, knowing only the baptism of John.

Apollos was a hard worker, he taught with much fervor.

See Paul's teaching meetings.

> **Acts 19:8** And he went into the synagogue, and spake boldly for the space of three months, disputing and persuading the things concerning the kingdom of God. **Vs 9** But when divers were hardened, and believed not, but spake evil of that way before the multitude, he departed from them, and separated the disciples, disputing daily in the school of one Tyrannus. **Vs 10** And this continued by the space of two years; so that all they which dwelt in Asia heard the word of the Lord Jesus, both Jews and Greeks.

This was almost three years of DAILY teaching.

Teaching takes work and time. You cannot call 25-30 mins Sunday sermons teaching! What were you explaining? My book of Bible stories? At least, one hour should be dedicated to teaching. Do not allow singing, announcements, special presentations etc. to becloud the major reason for Church meetings which is Bible study.

> **Acts 20:7** And upon the first day of the week, when the disciples came together to break bread, Paul preached unto them, ready to depart on the morrow; and continued his speech until midnight.

Paul taught from evening till midnight.

Then, we have the Eutychus story

> **Vs 11** When he therefore was come up again, and had broken bread, and eaten, and talked a long while, even till break of day, so he departed.

He taught till day break! Bible teaching should be given adequate attention. Believers need to be taught. Be ready to speak for long; take your time. If the day's meeting is not sufficient, break it into a series.

The effect of such labor is that it makes the teacher diligent and it disciplines the audience.

> **2nd Timothy 4:2** Preach the word; be instant in season, out of season; reprove, rebuke, exhort with

all longsuffering and doctrine. **Vs 3** For the time will come when they will not endure sound doctrine; but after their own lusts shall they heap to themselves teachers, having itching ears;

Be a hard worker. Teaching is hard work; the preparation and the act itself. Let us volunteer to learn, be taught and teach others!

Paul, Timothy and Titus (How to mentor younger ministers)

In instructing the younger minister, in this case; Timothy and Titus, Paul's major focus was preservation of truth, doctrine.

> **1 Timothy 1:3,10** As I besought thee to abide still at Ephesus, when I went into Macedonia, that thou mightest charge some that they teach no other doctrine, **Vs 10** For whoremongers, for them that defile themselves with mankind, for menstealers, for liars, for perjured persons, and if there be any other thing that is contrary to sound doctrine;

He instructed Timothy to ensure Scriptures are well interpreted and falsehood exposed.

> **1 Timothy 3:2** A bishop then must be ..., apt to teach;

A leader must be apt, able and skillful at teaching.

> **1 Timothy 4:1**Now the Spirit speaketh expressly, that in the latter times some shall depart from the faith, giving heed to seducing spirits, and doctrines of devils;

He warned against teachings...**diverse doctrine** and not

teaching itself

> **1 Timothy 4:6** If thou put the brethren in remembrance of these things, thou shalt be a good minister of Jesus Christ, nourished up in the words of faith and of good doctrine, whereunto thou hast attained.

Good doctrine

> **1 Timothy 4:13** Till I come, give attendance to reading, to exhortation, to doctrine.

Give attendance to teaching

> **1 Timothy 4:16** Take heed unto thyself, and unto the doctrine; continue in them: for in doing this thou shalt both save thyself, and them that hear thee.

To truly save the flock from all sorts of falsehood, give yourself to doctrine

> **1 Timothy 5:17** Let the elders that rule well be counted worthy of double honour, especially they who labour in the word and doctrine.

Elders are to seen teaching laboriously

> **1 Timothy 6:1,3** Let as many servants as are under the yoke count their own masters worthy of all

honour, that the name of God and his doctrine be not blasphemed. **Vs 3** If any man teach otherwise, and consent not to wholesome words, even the words of our Lord Jesus Christ, and to the doctrine which is according to godliness;

Doctrine must be preserved.

2 Timothy 1:13 Hold fast the form of sound words, which thou hast heard of me, in faith and love which is in Christ Jesus.

Hold fast to sound teaching

2 Timothy 2:2 And the things that thou hast heard of me among many witnesses, the same commit thou to faithful men, who shall be able to teach others also.

Commit these, to men who will teach them

2 Timothy 2:24-25 And the servant of the Lord must not strive; but be gentle unto all men, apt to teach, patient, **Vs 25** In meekness instructing those that oppose themselves; if God peradventure will give them repentance to the acknowledging of the truth;

The servant of God must be able to teach and correct others with sound doctrine

2 Timothy 3:16-17 All Scripture is given by inspiration of God, and is profitable for doctrine, for reproof, for correction, for instruction in righteousness: **Vs 17** That the man of God may be perfect, throughly furnished unto all good works.

All Scriptures are given for doctrine.

This says it all.

True doctrine is to rightly divide the word of truth not bulldoze your way with "stories and testimonies "called results

2 Timothy 2:15 Study to shew thyself approved unto God, a workman that needeth not to be ashamed, rightly dividing the word of truth.

This is the true test of a minister

2 Timothy 4:2 Preach the word; be instant in season, out of season; reprove, rebuke, exhort with all longsuffering and doctrine.

Even when men are not listening, do not go seeker sensitive, stick to the doctrine

Paul did and kept the faith, this refers to doctrine

2 Timothy 4:7 I have fought a good fight, I have finished my course, I have kept the faith:

The preponderance of emphasizing doctrine is so much to Timothy that it can't be underplayed today.

Same to Titus.

> **Titus 1:9** Holding fast the faithful word as he hath been taught, that he may be able by sound doctrine both to exhort and to convince the gainsayers.

He must hold fast, not give heed to falsehood or intimidation.

He must teach sound doctrine

> **Titus 2:1** But speak thou the things which become sound doctrine:

You can't sidestep the place of correct application of Scriptures, it's deadly and very misleading

Paul's relationship with Titus and Timothy had much to do with the common doctrine he taught and which they did too

> **Titus 2:2,7** That the aged men be sober, grave, temperate, sound in faith, in charity, in patience. **Vs 7** In all things shewing thyself a pattern of good works: in doctrine shewing uncorruptness, gravity, sincerity,

Also, elderly and young men

Titus 2:10 Not purloining, but shewing all good fidelity; that they may adorn the doctrine of God our Saviour in all things.

And for all too, we must adorn the doctrine of God.

We cannot claim to be meeting needs using Scriptures dishonestly.

That is utter nonsense.

2 Corinthians 4:2 But have renounced the hidden things of dishonesty, not walking in craftiness, nor handling the word of God deceitfully; but by manifestation of the truth commending ourselves to every man's conscience in the sight of God.

The ministry of the Church is built on teaching, properness of doctrine.

It saves the flock as Paul instructed Timothy.

This is the apostolic practice

Acts 2:42 And they continued stedfastly in the apostles' doctrine and fellowship, and in breaking of bread, and in prayers.

Steadfastly

Acts 11:26 And when he had found him, he brought him unto Antioch. And it came to pass, that a whole year they assembled themselves with the Church, and taught much people. And the disciples were called Christians first in Antioch.

They taught much people.

Last year during the Annual World Changers Conference (WCC) of the Church I serve as Pastor, which is organized for ministers I said "If what you refer to as results in ministry is crowd, money and real estate etc. you are an unwise"

I choose to repeat it again; If results of numbers, money, spread and societal influence are more important to you I suggest you either Learn "ministry" from:

Watch Tower Mission aka Jehovah's Witness

Started 1870 and has since spread worldwide
Membership - 8.2million
Yearly revenue -$950million (2001), they don't receive tithes.

Over $80million spent on missions annually
Branches -118,000 in 125 Nations
Bible in over 120 languages
Net worth- well above $40billion

Members include prime ministers of nations, presidents of multinational corporations etc.

Or

You learn ministry from

Church of Jesus Christ Latter Day Saints (Mormons)

Started since 1830

In 176 Nations
Membership -15 million
Branches -28,000
They have arguably one of the most exquisite brand of buildings for worship globally

Missionaries - 85,000
Donations to charity yearly -$100million
Net worth -over $80billion

The above cited "ministries" disrespect Bible interpretation yet have results to prove, with their error leading millions to destruction.

So, if you are bound by carnal things and not the truth revealed in Scriptures claiming it is not about doctrine but "results" I have a more viable example for you to follow.

Anyone telling you doctrine is not important disrespects Paul and the apostles and is either ignorant or dishonest and those who cheered such heretic influence are either stupid or brainwashed.

2 Timothy 2:15 Study to shew thyself approved unto God, a workman that needeth not to be ashamed, rightly dividing the word of truth.

True mentoring is focused on doctrine not crowds that can be surpassed at Emirates stadium or the Hajj or property that the world has in countless numbers

Titus 2:1 But speak thou the things which become sound doctrine:

The gospel reaches crowds but does not use error to do this.

You must set your sail and beware of not being diligent with the Scriptures in the bid to acquire wealth and influence as some do

Heed Paul's counsel

1 Timothy 6:9-11 But they that will be rich fall into temptation and a snare, and into many foolish and hurtful lusts, which drown men in destruction and perdition. **Vs 10** For the love of money is the root of all evil: which while some coveted after, they have erred from the faith, and pierced themselves through with many sorrows. **Vs 11** But thou, O man of God, flee these things; and follow after righteousness, godliness, faith, love, patience, meekness.

Stay on course

God will cause increase in your work and supply your needs without you comprising the truth of His word

Study, pray and contend for the supernatural as you reach out to the lost with the gospel of His son no more

No hurries, no hastes, let the future birth itself!

What do You Believe?

I had a discussion with a younger minister who pastors in Lagos, Nigeria.

After our lengthy talk, I saw a need for much more reorientation of what ministry is for younger ministers like me too.

The one High point of our discussion was his library, full of all sorts of books by various authors, most of whose only assent was that "Jesus is our Saviour", in fact how this is, is hardly agreed with by most.

He is surely a product of a dysfunctional system I witnessed growing up too.

You attend a Christian program filled with several speakers with varying and contradictory teachings,

The idea back then was, just get results!

We then saw a generation who got results of crowds, massive structures, miracles, most of which were by trial and error, hit and miss.

Many or even most I knew and still know have no regular or consistent theology. Nothing systematic. Nothing definite.

If what's reigning is wisdom, everyone preached it... deliverance, anointing etc. Just to name a few,

Sad to say, many were half baked doctrinally and made every attempt to dissuade emphasis on correct Bible interpretation.

They were quick to call such things "doctrines" and its teachers "theologians".

Isn't that interesting?

In Paul's letters to Titus and Timothy, doctrine / teaching was arguably his most quoted word.

It is not unfounded to hear men whom we must still hold in high regard, despite this, we hear them make absolutely incredible statements

- Hear this "when faith fails, you trust God. Trust will never fail"

This is obviously made either in ignorance or deceit, I believe the former.

Yet, many will hear this and affirm it because he has a large Church etc.

Now, before proceeding, I frown and am wary of ministries who preach either consciously or unconsciously against numerical growth and influence.

If you are not pursuing numerical growth, then you do not have Christs Vision

God gives increase. He said "all nations, all the world"

That's huge.

However, we must be careful how we do this.

Paul warns;

> **1 Corinthians 3:10** ... But let every man take heed how he buildeth thereupon.

Not at the cost of truth. Do not sacrifice the doctrine of Christ for growth.

Again, we had a generation that was not mentored in doctrine hence cannot mentor anyone with such.

I shudder when I hear of Church growth conferences, many are full of non-biblical opinions.

Again, the same trial and error versions. Be careful! You cannot give what you do not have

Let me track back a little.

In the 1970s and 1980s the **SU** (Scripture union) did a great job earlier on but somewhat a revival came that swept its relevance away.

It seemed proponents of that revival felt the SU were too rigid etc.

In fact, it was nicknamed **"suegbe union"** (**suegbe** means "**slow**" in Yoruba language)

They might have been right about some of its emphasis; sounding legalistic etc.

But again, we often throw away the baby with the bath water.

With this came a contempt for Bible teaching, study, school etc.

In fact, since most leading persona then hardly had formal Bible and ministerial training, there went out of the window the need for systematic theology.

Such revival though of God but since men always were stewards of God's move had the evident traits of human bias and weakness.

Correct Bible interpretation was thrashed.

A great number could not handle simple "Rightly dividing" of Scriptures.

No distinction or grasp of the Old Testament and New Testament,

Understanding the Epistles looked like rocket science.

Since as it were, the crowds then were pulled because of other spiritual things besides spiritual growth, seeming Churches with Bible study emphasis had whittled down influence.

I must note however, that a Church stood out (amongst many others which must have too)

Deeper life Bible Church.

It had the largest single congregation in Africa.

And this was from Bible study meetings.

You may not accept several things taught but you sure saw a diligence with Scriptures.

As the revival continued, more programs, events had to be held to sustain the crowds.

This is still the model today!

Since many had no clue about discipleship which only happens by teaching, they could only give what they had

It was not difficult for success motivation to gain ground.

Since no foundation was built, things kept being re-done.

Gradually, you could not tell a believer from others. Even a preacher of Christ from others. We all sounded alike.

Discernment is only available when there is sound teaching

> **Ephesians 4:13-14** Till we all come in the unity of the faith, and of the knowledge of the Son of God, unto a perfect man, unto the measure of the stature of the fulness of Christ: **Vs 14** That we henceforth be no more children, tossed to and fro, and carried about with every wind of doctrine, by the sleight of men, and cunning craftiness, whereby they lie in wait to deceive;

To and fro, this is the experience of trying to get results from reading after men of different persuasions but your motivation is just success.

It was not difficult to grow Churches without prayer and evangelism.

Just do what everyone does.

Once again, the word will bring increase no doubt but painstakingly, gradually and with the supernatural too.

Why am I saying this?

Because I am involved. This revival needs another revival.

Since we jettisoned Sunday schools for convenience.

First service 45 minutes etc. now the vogue.

We shortened services, particularly the sermons for more praise worship, less prayers. In fact, many sermons are not Bible teachings, rather seeker friendly meetings,

We have invited trouble.

- Mixed multitudes.
- Prayerlessness.
- Absence of spiritual growth.

I honour that generation. I learnt a whole lot from it and will be forever indebted.

I mean forever.

Grace received too. Hands were laid on me through it and it left indelible marks on me.

However, it is pertinent, it cannot go beyond its limits.

Hence, I do not hold many responsible for these issues.

To continue with these imperfections will be insanity.

Before you start a Church, what do you believe?

Who taught you?

What training do you have?

Have you taken time to fully learn doctrine?

> **2 Timothy 3:10** But thou hast fully known my doctrine, manner of life, purpose, faith, longsuffering, charity, patience,

Or you want to use the flock as testing grounds?

If this is not done, you will use the same templates above discussed

Plenty programs, numerous speakers.

Use them to grow Church,

Study what big Churches are doing and copy it.

But let me warn you!

The time span for that vogue is thinning out.

It is in its last lap.

You must grow up spiritually. You must be well grounded in God's word.

Find a pastor or teacher you will learn fully under! Not fishing around for doctrines etc.

If closing a work to do this will help, please do!

Stop trying to replicate programs done by others.

Did you hear from God?

Someone tried to replicate our meetings and I laughed out loud, will he replicate the Grace too?

Has he been trained?

Or again, it is just as we have pointed out, just doing what should work!

Dear fellow minister.

Take these words as brotherly counsel.

Those who made these lapses were not in error, as many of them did not know any better.

You might be shocked they would not be judged for them.

But see, you have no excuse! Do not be in a hurry to grow a Church.

Be in a hurry to grow spiritually if you will be in haste at all.

How's your spiritual life? Bible study? Prayer life? Can you do evangelism? Do you know how to take notes? Have you been taught how to preach and teach?

Please find out!

A fresh generation is emerging; The Word of God; well taught, received and understood. The Spirit in awesome demonstration.

Walking in love is our culture, prayer is our dependence; we know to be led by the spirit not vogues and the Church growing spiritually and numerically.

Kingdom

1st Samuel 8:5 And said unto him, Behold, thou art old, and thy sons walk not in thy ways: now make us a king to judge us like all the nations. **Vs 6** But the thing displeased Samuel, when they said, Give us a king to judge us. And Samuel prayed unto the LORD **Vs 7** And the LORD said unto Samuel, Hearken unto the voice of the people in all that they say unto thee: for they have not rejected thee, but they have rejected me, that I should not reign over them.

This story explains the history of kings and rulers in Israel.

Moses had earlier spoken of God's plans,

> **Exodus 19:5** Now therefore, if ye will obey my voice indeed, and keep my covenant, then ye shall be a peculiar treasure unto me above all people: for all the earth *is* mine: **Vs 6** And ye shall be unto me a kingdom of priests, and an holy nation. These *are* the words which thou shalt speak unto the children of Israel.

He partially unveiled God's plan for His Church.

Peter did speak as well,

> **1ˢᵗ Peter 2:9** But ye *are* a chosen generation, a royal priesthood, an holy nation, a peculiar people; that ye should shew forth the praises of him who hath called you out of darkness into his marvellous light: **Vs 10** Which in time past *were* not a people, but *are*

now the people of God: which had not obtained mercy, but now have obtained mercy.

All believers are kings and priests.

Revelation 5:10 And hast made us unto our God kings and priests: and we shall reign on the earth.

Paul equally teaches this differently,

Romans 5:17 For if by one man's offence death reigned by one; much more they which receive abundance of grace and of the gift of righteousness shall reign in life by one, Jesus Christ.)

"Reign" means "be kings". It is taken from the words "dominion" and "kingdom".

Ephesians 1:21 Far above all principality, and power, and might, and dominion, and every name that is named, not only in this world, but also in that which is to come: **Vs 22** And hath put all *things* under his feet, and gave him *to be* the head over all *things* to the Church, **Vs 23** Which is his body, the fulness of him that filleth all in all.

This is the kingdom; sitting in Christ. It is not in an office of a conglomerate or a political position.

Scriptures ALWAYS differentiates the two.

Just like Samuel told Israel, Jesus told us too.

> **Matthew 12:28** But if I cast out devils by the Spirit of God, then the kingdom of God is come unto you.

He mentions casting out Devils.

> **Luke 17:20** And when he was demanded of the Pharisees, when the kingdom of God should come, he answered them and said, The kingdom of God cometh not with observation: **Vs 21** Neither shall they say, Lo here! or, lo there! for, behold, the kingdom of God is within you.

It is not by buildings or structures; Christ is the kingdom.

He told Pilate the same.

> **John 18:36** Jesus answered, My kingdom is not of this world: if my kingdom were of this world, then would my servants fight, that I should not be delivered to the Jews: but now is my kingdom not from hence. **Vs 37** Pilate therefore said unto him, Art thou a king then? Jesus answered, Thou sayest that I am a king. To this end was I born, and for this cause

came I into the world, that I should bear witness unto the truth. Every one that is of the truth heareth my voice.

It is neither in the commercial nor political world. It does not involve soldiers and human sophistry and structures.

Jesus never asked anyone in his days to desire governmental powers. He did not preach a kingdom takeover.

Rather, he makes a distinction.

> **Matthew 20:25** But Jesus called them *unto him,* and said, Ye know that the princes of the Gentiles exercise dominion over them, and they that are great exercise authority upon them. **Vs 26** But it shall not be so among you: but whosoever will be great among you, let him be your minister; **Vs 27** And whosoever will be chief among you, let him be your servant: **Vs 28** Even as the Son of man came not to be ministered unto, but to minister, and to give his life a ransom for many.

His kingdom is in His love, not ruling others with the influence of material acquisition or positions. It is to serve. That service is love.

The rich and poor, young and old, great and small can function in this.

Later on, Peter was still mistaken.

> **Acts 1:6** When they therefore were come together, they asked of him, saying, Lord, wilt thou at this time restore again the kingdom to Israel? **Vs 7** And he said unto them, It is not for you to know the times or the seasons, which the Father hath put in his own power. **Vs 8** But ye shall receive power, after that the Holy Ghost is come upon you: and ye shall be witnesses unto me both in Jerusalem, and in all Judaea, and in Samaria, and unto the uttermost part of the earth.

Jesus told him that his kingdom had nothing to do with upstaging the Roman Empire.

Earlier, Peter wanted the kingdom Israel desired, that is, controlling resources, media, men, finances etc. Peter spoke foolishly. God's kingdom is not things.

Paul was very clear.

> **Romans 14:17** For the kingdom of God is not meat and drink; but righteousness, and peace, and joy in the Holy Ghost. **Vs 18** For he that in these things

serveth Christ *is* acceptable to God, and approved of men. **Vs 19** Let us therefore follow after the things which make for peace, and things wherewith one may edify another.

It is not in things but in the Spirit; things of the spirit.

Jesus taught his disciples this too.

Matthew 16:18 And I say also unto thee, That thou art Peter, and upon this rock I will build my Church; and the gates of hell shall not prevail against it. **Vs 19** And I will give unto thee the keys of the kingdom of heaven: and whatsoever thou shalt bind on earth shall be bound in heaven: and whatsoever thou shalt loose on earth shall be loosed in heaven.

You loose and bind. Then, it happens in heaven; in the spirit.

Notice that it is not physical. It shall be in heaven. Heaven means non - material. This includes all things spiritual.

However, it includes things many folks do not consider.

He uses the same later on settling disputes.

Matthew 18:15 Moreover if thy brother shall trespass against thee, go and tell him his fault between thee and him alone: if he shall hear thee, thou hast gained thy brother. **Vs 16** But if he will not hear *thee, then* take with thee one or two more, that in the mouth of two or three witnesses every word may be established. **Vs 17** And if he shall neglect to hear them, tell *it* unto the Church: but if he neglect to hear the Church, let him be unto thee as an heathen man and a publican. **Vs 18** Verily I say unto you, Whatsoever ye shall bind on earth shall be bound in heaven: and whatsoever ye shall loose on earth shall be loosed in heaven. **Vs 19** Again I say unto you, That if two of you shall agree on earth as touching any thing that they shall ask, it shall be done for them of my Father which is in heaven. **Vs 20** For where two or three are gathered together in my name, there am I in the midst of them.

If a brother refuses reconciliation after you go to him, others and then you tell it to the Church, what are we to bind and loose? What will be done by the father? What are two or three gathered in this name for?

Matthew 18:21 Then came Peter to him, and said, Lord, how oft shall my brother sin against me, and I forgive him? till seven times? **Vs 22** Jesus saith unto him, I say not unto thee, Until seven times: but, Until seventy times seven.

Forgiveness!

Hence, "we bind and loose" means "we decide and allow".

Jesus says "seven times seventy"! That is the fathers will; the kingdom of God.

We rose from the dead with Christ and are now in Him.

> **Ephesians 2:5** Even when we were dead in sins, hath quickened us together with Christ, (by grace ye are saved;) **Vs 6** And hath raised *us* up together, and made *us* sit together in heavenly *places* in Christ Jesus:

Hence, we walk in this reality.

We moved from one kingdom into another.

> **Colossians 1:12** Giving thanks unto the Father, which hath made us meet to be partakers of the inheritance of the saints in light: **Vs 13** Who hath delivered us from the power of darkness, and hath translated *us* into the kingdom of his dear Son: **Vs 14** In whom we have redemption through his blood, *even* the forgiveness of sins:

This is nothing earthly, not politics or commerce. This kingdom is in men's hearts not offices.

> **Ephesians 2:2** Wherein in time past ye walked according to the course of this world, according to the prince of the power of the air, the spirit that now worketh in the children of disobedience: **Vs 3** Among whom also we all had our conversation in times past in the lusts of our flesh, fulfilling the

desires of the flesh and of the mind; and were by nature the children of wrath, even as others.

Desires and conduct; not positions and structures.

Now we are in this kingdom. We forgive others.

Ephesians 4:32 And be ye kind one to another, tenderhearted, forgiving one another, even as God for Christ's sake hath forgiven you.

Love! We walk in it.

Ephesians 5:1 Be ye therefore followers of God, as dear children; **Vs 2** And walk in love, as Christ also hath loved us, and hath given himself for us an offering and a sacrifice to God for a sweetsmelling savour.

Also, our conflict is spiritual and not with men, not hustling or haggling for positions and influence.

Ephesians 6:10 Finally, my brethren, be strong in the Lord, and in the power of his might. **Vs 11** Put on the whole armour of God, that ye may be able to stand against the wiles of the devil. **Vs 12** For we wrestle not against flesh and blood, but against principalities, against powers, against the rulers of the darkness of this world, against spiritual wickedness in high *places.* **Vs 13** Wherefore take unto you the whole armour of God, that ye may be able to withstand in the evil day, and having done all, to stand. **Vs 14** Stand therefore, having your loins girt about with truth, and having on the breastplate of righteousness; **Vs 15** And your feet shod with the preparation of the gospel of peace; **Vs 16** Above all, taking the shield of faith, wherewith ye shall be able to quench all the fiery darts of the wicked. **Vs 17** And take the helmet of salvation, and the sword of the Spirit, which is the word of God: **Vs 18** Praying always with all prayer and supplication in the Spirit, and watching thereunto with all perseverance and supplication for all saints;

This is very clear.

It is not by becoming the president of a nation or owning business empires.

Hence the prophecy of David,

> **Psalms 110:1** The LORD said unto my Lord, Sit thou at my right hand, until I make thine enemies thy footstool.

David knew he never occupied God's kingdom. He had man's kingdom, resources, buildings, organizations, influence but not the kingdom.

He looked forward to God's kingdom.

Matthew 22:42 Saying, What think ye of Christ? whose son is he? They say unto him, *The Son* of David. **Vs 43** He saith unto them, How then doth David in spirit call him Lord, saying, **Vs 44** The LORD said unto my Lord, Sit thou on my right hand, till I make thine enemies thy footstool? **Vs 45** If David then call him Lord, how is he his son?

Christ was the first king in this kingdom.

Not earthly influence!

John 6:15 When Jesus therefore perceived that they would come and take him by force, to make him a king, he departed again into a mountain himself alone.

Jesus rejected this.

This kingdom happened upon his resurrection.

Acts 2:33 Therefore being by the right hand of God exalted, and having received of the Father the promise of the Holy Ghost, he hath shed forth this, which ye now see and hear. **Vs 34** For David is not ascended into the heavens: but he saith himself, The LORD said unto my Lord, Sit thou on my right hand, **Vs 35** Until I make thy foes thy footstool.
Vs 36 Therefore let all the house of Israel know assuredly, that God hath made that same Jesus, whom ye have crucified, both Lord and Christ.

Paul teaches that this will be consummated.

> **1ˢᵗ Corintians 15:24** Then *cometh* the end, when he shall have delivered up the kingdom to God, even the Father; when he shall have put down all rule and all authority and power. **Vs 25** For he must reign, till he hath put all enemies under his feet. **Vs 26** The last enemy *that* shall be destroyed *is* death**. Vs 27** For he hath put all things under his feet. But when he saith all things are put under *him, it is* manifest that he is excepted, which did put all things under him.

Nothing money, education, politics or commerce can do.

This is the kingdom.

We must never think otherwise. Else, like Israel, we would be rejecting His kingdom in Christ for our kingdom in this world.

> **1ˢᵗ Corinthians 2:6** Howbeit we speak wisdom among them that are perfect: yet not the wisdom of this world, nor of the princes of this world, that come to nought: **Vs 8** Which none of the princes of this world knew: for had they known *it,* they would not have crucified the Lord of glory.

Not science, commerce, technology, politics.

Salvation in Christ is available to ALL.

ON PERSECUTIONS

Acts 28:3 And when Paul had gathered a bundle of sticks, and laid them on the fire, there came a viper out of the heat, and fastened on his hand. **Vs 4** And when the barbarians saw the venomous beast hang on his hand, they said among themselves, No doubt this man is a murderer, whom, though he hath escaped the sea, yet vengeance suffereth not to live.

There are several times ministers of the word are so badly branded by men, based on certain experiences they have or have had and mostly via wrong perception.

Here Paul was deemed to be suffering for not being of God.

Ministry comes with its warts and farts. We are dealing with men

Many times, not on ordinary terms

> **Ephesians 2:2** Wherein in time past ye walked according to the course of this world, according to the prince of the power of the air, the spirit that now worketh in the children of disobedience:

Men in positions of influence, and such have spiritual connotations with natural interface

> **Ephesians 6:12** For we wrestle not against flesh and blood, but against principalities, against powers, against the rulers of the darkness of this world, against spiritual wickedness in high places.

Truth be said, these texts speak of unbelievers. But believers who are given to strife will act the same way.

> **1 Corinthians 3:3** For ye are yet carnal: for whereas there is among you envying, and strife, and divisions, are ye not carnal, and walk as men?

They will act like the unsaved and their approach might not be so different.

> **Ephesians 4:26-27** Be ye angry, and sin not: let not the sun go down upon your wrath:

Vs 27 Neither give place to the devil.

Believers do yield to the devil.

1 Timothy 5:15 For some are already turned aside after Satan.

Even leaders.

Paul's challenge at Jerusalem was such.

Acts 21:20-21 And when they heard it, they glorified the Lord, and said unto him, Thou seest, brother, how many thousands of Jews there are which believe; and they are all zealous of the law: **Vs 21** And they are informed of thee, that thou teachest all the Jews which are among the Gentiles to forsake Moses, saying that they ought not to circumcise their children, neither to walk after the customs.

His opponents were believers. Legalistic brethren, just like the law, are harsh towards the gospel.

When this happens, the proponents build impressions into the minds of their followers.

2 Corinthians 10:3-5 For though we walk in the flesh, we do not war after the flesh: **Vs 4** (For the weapons of our warfare are not carnal, but mighty through God to the pulling down of strong holds;) **Vs**

5 Casting down imaginations, and every high thing that exalteth itself against the knowledge of God, and bringing into captivity every thought to the obedience of Christ;

Paul's teaching here was not about some demons but a knowledge system that opposes the word. It is in men's minds.

Some will not want to hear the doctrine of eternal salvation because of what they had been told, others will not want to listen to a preacher for what they had been   told.
They will not even be given the room for objective reasoning.

I don't reply such folks, I just increase what I am doing

Hence the need for the minister of the word to never resort to the flesh; "PR", Branding, etc.

Just stay in the spirit. Preach, teach and Pray!

Ephesians 6:17-18 And take the helmet of salvation, and the sword of the Spirit, which is the word of God: **Vs 18** Praying always with all prayer and supplication in the Spirit, and watching thereunto with all perseverance and supplication for all saints;

The sword of the spirit is praying always in tongues.

Hence I pray much more!

Ministry will always come with its own heat, Jesus had false reports about what he taught

> **Matthew 26:59-60** Now the chief priests, and elders, and all the council, sought false witness against Jesus, to put him to death; **Vs 60** But found none: yea, though many false witnesses came, yet found they none. At the last came two false witnesses,

They scrutinized his teachings to find something against him. They tried to use folks who attended his meetings, it failed still.

Then finally

> **Matthew 26:61** And said, This fellow said, I am able to destroy the temple of God, and to build it in three days. **Vs 62** And the high priest arose, and said unto him, Answerest thou nothing? what is it which these witness against thee?

They twist his words to say he was attacking Pastor X or Archbishop Y

That's their ilk and pattern

> **1 Corinthians 3:4** For while one saith, I am of Paul; and another, I am of Apollos; are ye not carnal?

It is about men for them, and they will rope in anything to accomplish the evil work.

Who is Pastor X or Bishop Y? Aren't they God's servants?

1 Corinthians 3:5 Who then is Paul, and who is Apollos, but ministers by whom ye believed, even as the Lord gave to every man?

Matthew 26:64 Jesus saith unto him, Thou hast said: nevertheless I say unto you, Hereafter shall ye see the Son of man sitting on the right hand of power, and coming in the clouds of heaven.

As he spoke, they were more incensed.

That is the thing with opponents, nothing you say will matter. They wanted Jesus to appear like he had been contemptuous of the law and its priests and eventually God

> **John 18:23** Jesus answered him, If I have spoken evil, bear witness of the evil: but if well, why smitest thou me?

Did he speak the truth? Yes! But since it affected their fiefdom, he had to be taken out.

They called Jesus a blasphemer, a liar! But generally believed.

They achieved this by putting his teachings against personalities, and made it sound like what it never was.

They did the same to Paul;

> **Acts 21:28** Crying out, Men of Israel, help: This is the man, that teacheth all men every where against the people, and the law, and this place: and further brought Greeks also into the temple, and hath polluted this holy place.

They will rally crowds against you; they will use the media; TV, conferences, Facebook. To make men not listen to you.

Paul ensured they never stopped him. In fact in the presence of the authorities he gave one of the most daring teachings in the book of acts

> **Acts 26:18** To open their eyes, and to turn them from darkness to light, and from the power of Satan unto God, that they may receive forgiveness of sins, and inheritance among them which are sanctified by faith that is in me... **Vs 22** Having therefore obtained help of God, I continue unto this day, witnessing both to small and great, saying none other things than those which the prophets and Moses did say should come: **Vs 23** That Christ should suffer, and that he should be the first that should rise from the

dead, and should shew light unto the people, and to the Gentiles.

Paul was so persuasive, Felix had to scream;

Acts 26:24 And as he thus spake for himself, Festus said with a loud voice, Paul, thou art beside thyself; much learning doth make thee mad.

That's the power of conviction.

We do not compromise for acceptance, platforms to speak or "doors"!

Paul went further

Acts 26:25 But he said, I am not mad, most noble Festus; but speak forth the words of truth and soberness. **Vs 26** For the king knoweth of these things, before whom also I speak freely: for I am persuaded that none of these things are hidden from him; for this thing was not done in a corner. **Vs 27**King Agrippa, believest thou the prophets? I know that thou believest.

Such gusto, such grit of conviction.

The king had to comment too

Acts 26:28 Then Agrippa said unto Paul, Almost thou persuadest me to be a Christian.

Glory!

Paul quipped further

> **Acts 26:29** And Paul said, I would to God, that not only thou, but also all that hear me this day, were both almost, and altogether such as I am, except these bonds.

This is not being seeker sensitive, this was his message! This Means, no letting up; No backing out. Put the word out, they will hear it in their bedrooms.

Thank God for technology. You do not need a skyscraper cathedral to reach thousands and millions of men, rather find every media and put it there!

God's word is not bound!

> **2nd Timothy 2:9** Wherein I suffer trouble, as an evil doer, even unto bonds; but the word of God is not bound.

No matter what they call your ministry, do not allow anyone to stop your work. If some Churches, ministers or some believers do not receive you, others will.

> **Matthew 10:14** And whosoever shall not receive you, nor hear your words, when ye depart out of that house or city, shake off the dust of your feet.

Never allow anyone stop your momentum!

Speaking evil of ministers of the word is legendary. It did not just start.

Paul spoke of this too

> **2 Corinthians 6:8** By honour and dishonour, by evil report and good report: as deceivers, and yet true; **Vs 9** As unknown, and yet well known; as dying, and, behold, we live; as chastened, and not killed;

Keep your eyes on the ball. Stay full of the word and prayer.

No amount of diplomacy convinces opponents of the message. Be more aggressive.

Ensure you are not getting personal with anyone, do not get rude or petulant. Speak the truth in love;

> **Ephesians 4:15** But speaking the truth in love, may grow up into him in all things, which is the head, even Christ:

This is not diplomacy or hypocrisy

> **Romans 12:9** Let love be without dissimulation. Abhor that which is evil; cleave to that which is good.

Love detests false doctrines, it is not hypocrisy (dissimulation).

Hence the context of speaking the truth in love is to

prevent false teachers.

> **Ephesians 4:14** That we henceforth be no more children, tossed to and fro, and carried about with every wind of doctrine, by the sleight of men, and cunning craftiness, whereby they lie in wait to deceive;

Many who mouth "speak the truth in love" do not even know what it means! Never mind them. But stay focused on your work. And just like Paul in Melita, things will turn around much later

> **Acts 28:10** Who also honoured us with many honours; and when we departed, they laded us with such things as were necessary. **Vs 23** And when they had appointed him a day, there came many to him into his lodging; to whom he expounded and testified the kingdom of God, persuading them concerning Jesus, both out of the law of Moses, and out of the prophets, from morning till evening. **Vs 30**And Paul dwelt two whole years in his own hired house, and received all that came in unto him, **Vs 31** Preaching the kingdom of God, and teaching those things which concern the Lord Jesus Christ, with all confidence, no man forbidding him.

Like E.W. Kenyon who was labeled a heretic in his days,

yet his books have brought the revelation of Christ's redemption and the new creation to the Church more than anyone in the 20th century.

He kept writing, and never waned. I encourage you as I do me.

> **1 Corinthians 15:58** Therefore, my beloved brethren, be ye stedfast, unmoveable, always abounding in the work of the Lord, forasmuch as ye know that your labour is not in vain in the Lord.

ON PATIENCE

A conversation ensued between myself and a younger minister a few years back.

I asked him if there are things "good desire and faith" could kill. Seeing he was so passionate about reaching out, ministry, he seemed to want things done "ASAP".

He answered "I don't know sir"

I quipped "but Scriptures teach all things are possible?"

Then I asked him, "if his faith and desire can limit the length of pregnancy to say 1 hour, such that between conception and delivery, the entire process takes 1 hour".

He looked at me in amazement, and answered; "that would be too premature"

Excellent!

Jesus taught that the word works with time

> **Matthew 13:23** But he that received seed into the good ground is he that heareth the word, and understandeth it; which also beareth fruit, and bringeth forth, some an hundredfold, some sixty, some thirty.

Sixty, thirty and hundred are gradual stages, hundred being the completion.

> **Luke 8:15** But that on the good ground are they, which in an honest and good heart, having heard the word, keep it, and bring forth fruit with patience.

Patience means - PATIENCE!

> **Mark 4:28** For the earth bringeth forth fruit of herself; first the blade, then the ear, after that the full corn in the ear.

Observe;

First the blade, then the ear, after that the full corn!

Process!

Same way you do not desire an unripe fruit or a premature baby, we must not desire hastily formed ministries and believers.

There is nothing in the fruit of the spirit called haste.

> **Galatians 5:19** Now the works of the flesh are manifest, which are these; Adultery, fornication, uncleanness, lasciviousness,

Lascivious means without regulation, it is a work of the flesh. Rather so much regulation exists in our spirit.

Gentleness, temperance, long suffering, meekness, peace and even the fruit itself, love are ALL measured and controlled lifestyles.

We are in a generation of haste.

Haste to know, read, talk, preach, start and sadly too, haste to stop!

Do you read patiently?

I have seen too many ask questions of things I post on social media, yet the answer is right there!!!

They are just in a hurry.

So many will also ask for quick answers to things, I usually say "go listen to so and so teaching" Some do not like it. It will demand time!

Others do and they are better for it.

Too many young ministers love to quickly open a website, put their teachings, blast on Facebook, and send links around.

Nothing wrong, but are you considering the fact that just a year or two ago you probably did not know what you are "blasting"?

Why not be patient.

Paul admonished Timothy about ordaining ministers

> **1 Timothy 5:22** Lay hands suddenly on no man, neither be partaker of other men's sins: keep thyself pure.

Be patient before choosing men into leadership.

Why the hurry to start a Church? Get on air, broadcast your services?

Some will claim "the world needs to hear the message"

Very true, but it still must not be done without the **word**.

You cannot desire to preach the word outside the word.

Too many are in a rat race for prominence, hence the haste to hold Bible school, school of ministry.

Imagine a very young minister (barely 3-5 years in ministry) writing to "fellow ministers"

At what age? Why the hurry?

> **1 Peter 5:5** Likewise, ye younger, submit yourselves unto the elder. Yea, all of you be subject one to another, and be clothed with humility: for God resisteth the proud, and giveth grace to the humble.

Peter writes here to younger ministers, there are younger elders.

Now, Back to our major theme.

Things that last, take time.

I had been put under pressure since the 1990s to write a book.

I told my encouragers, give me time.

I did not publish till over twenty years in Ministry, and it was never lack of audiences, finances or what to write.

You do not have to do this, just telling my own experiences.

Time creates depth, accuracy, originality, precision and most importantly, maturity.

Do not be quick to want to be known or quick to teach

new things.

> **Proverbs 29:20** Seest thou a man that is hasty in his words? there is more hope of a fool than of him.

You will end up being more foolish than a fool.

James so admonished too

> **James 1:19-20** Wherefore, my beloved brethren, let every man be swift to hear, slow to speak, slow to wrath: **Vs 20** For the wrath of man worketh not the righteousness of God.

Be slow.

I learnt this from Kenneth E. Hagin

"It is better to be slower than God than be ahead of him"

Accuracy and precision is better than speed.

The social media age is a quick fix, but very dangerous.

It is make believe, falsehood and pretense glorified.

Young folks trying to quickly showcase their exploits, some even put out videos for show off, with twists and turns.

Why?

Well, things done hurriedly might require lies,

exaggeration to make up for its inadequacies.

Some who Pastor today, should have waited longer. They know it.

God does things in His own time,

Paul was spoken to in **Acts 9**;

> **Acts 9:15-16** But the Lord said unto him, Go thy way: for he is a chosen vessel unto me, to bear my name before the Gentiles, and kings, and the children of Israel: **Vs 16** For I will shew him how great things he must suffer for my name's sake.

Yet, well over 10 years after.

> **Acts 13:2** As they ministered to the Lord, and fasted, the Holy Ghost said, Separate me Barnabas and Saul for the work whereunto I have called them.

Note; "**I have called**", not **"I will call"**, they just entered what had been on ground.

What is the difference?

Time!

Things take time.

Even after this

> **Acts 16:6-7** Now when they had gone throughout

Phrygia and the region of Galatia, and were forbidden of the Holy Ghost to preach the word in Asia, **Vs 7** After they were come to Mysia, they assayed to go into Bithynia: but the Spirit suffered them not.

They were forbidden to go to where they were called to!

They went later

Acts 19:10 And this continued by the space of two years; so that all they which dwelt in Asia heard the word of the Lord Jesus, both Jews and Greeks.

And things happened in two years. Two years? Not exactly.

Two years after **several years** of waiting and preparing.

In the midst of the wait, they went to Macedonia.

Acts 16:10 And after he had seen the vision, immediately we endeavoured to go into Macedonia, assuredly gathering that the Lord had called us for to preach the gospel unto them... **Vs 12** And from thence to Philippi, which is the chief city of that part of Macedonia, and a colony: and we were in that city abiding certain days.

Same places he got most ministry and financial support

2nd Corinthians 8:1 Moreover, brethren, we do you

to wit of the grace of God bestowed on the Churches of Macedonia; **Vs 2** How that in a great trial of affliction the abundance of their joy and their deep poverty abounded unto the riches of their liberality. **Vs 3** For to their power, I bear record, yea, and beyond their power they were willing of themselves;

Because of patience, the ministry received much help

They even gave their lives.

2nd Corinthians 8:5 And this they did , not as we hoped, but first gave their own selves to the Lord, and unto us by the will of God.

Philippians 4:15 Now ye Philippians know also, that in the beginning of the gospel, when I departed from Macedonia, no Church communicated with me as concerning giving and receiving, but ye only.

Do you know that it was during this period that he met some of his most arguably supportive folks.

<u>For example:</u>

Priscilla and Aquila

Acts 18:2 And found a certain Jew named Aquila, born in Pontus, lately come from Italy, with his wife Priscilla; (because that Claudius had commanded all Jews to depart from Rome:) and came unto them.

See what he called them in the book of Romans.

> **Romans 16:3** Greet Priscilla and Aquila my helpers in Christ Jesus: **Vs 4** Who have for my life laid down their own necks: unto whom not only I give thanks, but also all the Churches of the Gentiles.

That is the fruit of patience.

When we take our time, we follow God's plan, we shall find adequate resources, not necessarily material only to support us.

Haste will make you arrive at a distance quickly but not successfully, bruised, weak and unfulfilled.

In the absence of patience, we shall have quick fixes, very immature ministers and ministries, even with large numbers but no depth, no genuine identity.

Let me share a story

About Fifteen years ago, I was invited to attend a program organized by a young minister like me; A healing meeting

It was obvious, he was trying to copy a particular leading TV evangelist in Nigeria.

The branding, manner of taking testimonies etc. was so packaged,

So, the meeting ended, and did not have the kind of spectacular results expected.

I for one was not disappointed, because we might have the workings of miracles but do not determine how and when they are received.

With my experience in ministering God's Miracles, way before this fellow, I gladly rejoiced at what we saw. He tried to put up a front, obviously hiding his dismissed expectations, which was misplaced. He left, and I left afterwards.

He called me two days after, sharing the testimonies of the meeting with me.

I wondered why, because I felt I was there both spiritually and physically.

Then he drops the bombshell..."Pastor Segs did you see the testimonies; blind eyes, deaf ears etc."

"You had gone, people were so blessed"

I responded in silence.

I did not leave till the door of the auditorium was shut!

Maybe they organized another that night, maybe people came back, maybe, maybe.

Years later, a lady told me of how she was made to

testify about a heart disease healed by the same man, whilst she was still sick of it.

She was made to do a scam and it was published. She did eventually get healed of it. But not under him.

It is funny till date the minister still does the same things.

He has grown in it and with it. Competition and haste.

Till date, he still hops after any thing that is in rave. I doubt if he will change.

When you ought to be in primary one and you are hastily, illegitimately taken to five, you will be in class five but will be a primary one boy in another's class

I counsel young ministers...No matter the "move of the spirit" and the facade of social media, do not have an exaggerated opinion of yourself.

Take your time.

Do not join "generation haste".

Why Bible school? Telecast? Planting Churches around? Fathering young ministers? Are you not young too?

You are still young!

You will end up a signboard, you won't get there but only show the way!

Like Solomon said

> **Ecclesiastes 3:11** He hath made every thing beautiful in his time.

Patience is still in our spirit. A requirement for ministry and life.

For me, I will rather be waiting on God than run ahead in assumption or presumption or haste.

Stay focused!

As a much younger preacher, I cannot forget the manner some more elderly preachers viewed us. Whilst it was true we had exuberance (but what else is expected from a teenager), it was disheartening seeing how you were easily despised and not even seen with God's grace. It appeared more like they expected you to fail.

However, one person who spoke heavy words to encourage me was Ross Tatro. He said, "Keep your focus and make sure you are growing, your voice will become distinct sooner or later." I had attended the AIM conference at LRA, 1994 where he spoke those words to me.

Also, while preaching for my friend Bolu Paul in 1996, brother Toks (Tokunbo Adejuwon) capped it all by saying "be steadfast, let nothing move you". He can never imagine what that meant then.

I have since learnt to never see younger folks differently. Yes, they will be exuberant (in fact, most I see today do not have a quarter of what we did back then) but I am here to correct and yet encourage them to be all God planned for them, and they should not be afraid to make mistakes and be corrected and still inspired.

I laughed when some folks of late were trying to play Voltrons for brother Toks over an alleged Whatsapp group spat, he actually saw himself as a younger person in those folks (things he had done worse as a younger person) and we both laughed over it saying "ours is to encourage, counsel not discourage" seeing we had passed that same phase before.

I cannot be found doing less to younger folks. I am a

product of strong encouragement and supportive words. I still am.

Hence, I say to you young minister, "Be focused, be steadfast; nothing dies in your hands, your voice will be heard.

A lesson from Yonggi Cho

David Yonggi Cho once told the story of how he used to pack his sermons full of philosophical studies, yet wowed his audience.

He had a lady who had tirelessly but unsuccessfully tried getting her hubby to Church meetings, then eventually the man (hubby) showed up.

After the service, Dr. Cho was so eager to meet with the man, and the following conversation ensued

"So glad to see you sir, how did you see the service?" Asked Dr. Cho

"Hmm, I had a horrible experience, could not wait for you to stop", replied the man

Why? Asked Dr. Cho, wondering maybe because he was not yet a Christian

"It was full of philosophy; elementary philosophy, I am a professor of philosophy", the man continued

Then he gave a final comment, I believe should cause any preacher think;

"Pastor, preach from the Bible, let us face our own philosophy!" concluded the man.

In my opinion, the last line is the takeaway.

If you know how unbelieving business men and academia laugh pastors to scorn looking at our approach to use their ideas to wow our Churches, you will stick to the words of eternal life!

Just like Paul taught

1 Corinthians 2:1-2,4-5 And I, brethren, when I came to you, came not with excellency of speech or of wisdom, declaring unto you the testimony of God. **Vs 2** For I determined not to know any thing among you, save Jesus Christ, and him crucified. **Vs 4** And my speech and my preaching was not with enticing words of man's wisdom, but in demonstration of the Spirit and of power: **Vs 5**That your faith should not stand in the wisdom of men, but in the power of God.

PARTING SHOTS

Hold unto these words;

Firstly, follow God's plan for your life; the leading of the Spirit

Acts 13:2,4 As they ministered to the Lord, and fasted, the Holy Ghost said, Separate me Barnabas and Saul for the work whereunto I have called them. **Vs 4** So they, being sent forth by the Holy Ghost, departed unto Seleucia; and from thence they sailed to Cyprus.

This is critical at the start.

Acts 16:6 Now when they had gone throughout Phrygia and the region of Galatia, and were forbidden of the Holy Ghost to preach the word in Asia,

As you proceed further

Acts 27:23-24 For there stood by me this night the angel of God, whose I am, and whom I serve, **Vs 24**

Saying, Fear not, Paul; thou must be brought before Caesar: and, lo, God hath given thee all them that sail with thee.

Even when things are rough. This helps you not to compete with anyone.

You will function in the place of grace and you will never have to be ambitious.

Romans 12:4 For as we have many members in one body, and all members have not the same office:

1 Corinthians 15:10 But by the grace of God I am what I am: and his grace which was bestowed upon me was not in vain; but I laboured more abundantly than they all: yet not I, but the grace of God which was with me.

Labour is vital, but laboring outside your office and ministry just to compete with others is sheer waste of effort.   .

Secondly, give yourself to prayer.

Observe Jesus.;

Luke 3:21 Now when all the people were baptized,

it came to pass, that Jesus also being baptized, and praying, the heaven was opened,

This was John's baptism.

Luke 5:16 And he withdrew himself into the wilderness, and prayed.

Even when the Miracles were much.

Matthew 26:36 Then cometh Jesus with them unto a place called Gethsemane, and saith unto the disciples, Sit ye here, while I go and pray yonder.

Till the very end.

Paul too.

Acts 9:11 And the Lord said unto him, Arise, and go into the street which is called Straight, and enquire in the house of Judas for one called Saul, of Tarsus: for, behold, he prayeth,

At   the   start
Acts 16:25 And at midnight Paul and Silas prayed, and sang praises unto God: and the prisoners heard them.

When things went wrong

2 Timothy 1:3 I thank God, whom I serve from my forefathers with pure conscience, that without ceasing I have remembrance of thee in my prayers night and day;

Night and day!

The apostles also said this to ward off distractions

> **Acts 6:4** But we will give ourselves continually to prayer, and to the ministry of the word.

Enough said.

Thirdly, study the Scriptures.

- Jesus did.
- Paul did.

Paul commended Timothy for this

> **2 Timothy 3:15,17** And that from a child thou hast known the holy Scriptures, which are able to make thee wise unto salvation through faith which is in Christ Jesus. **Vs 17**That the man of God may be perfect, throughly furnished unto all good works.

This is your message and must never be treated with Levity

Also, be sacrificial.

It is called ministry because you are serving not being served

> **Matthew 20:27-28** And whosoever will be chief among you, let him be your servant: **Vs 28** Even as the Son of man came not to be ministered unto, but to minister, and to give his life a ransom for many.

You cannot be ambitious and be a servant.

1 Corinthians 4:9 For I think that God hath set forth us the apostles last, as it were appointed to death: for we are made a spectacle unto the world, and to angels, and to men.

Such commitment!

A young minister must realize this. It will take away pride, arrogance, selfishness and ambitious pursuits from your ministry.

Never forget, labour within your ministry; the grace given to you.

Do not try duplicating what others are doing, it is time

wasting.

You will labour and run in vain!

FINAL WORDS

Paul's parting shot was not so inspiring

2nd Timothy 4:7 I have fought a good fight, I have finished my course, I have kept the faith:

That is all!

Fight! Course! Faith!

What about

- Feats and achievements?
- Presidents who come for prayer or are Church members?
- Universities built?
- Jets owned?
- Nations you have Churches?
- How many sons in ministry?

- Books published all over the nations?

What about words like,

- I rose to the top

- I am no more on ground level

- Exploits we achieved

It did not sound like Paul knew much "revelation".

However, I believe he must have kept the faith since his writings have stood out centuries over centuries, almost 2000 years, laying the fabrics of truth and verity.

These are worth more than "seeing you at the top"(whatever this means).

When all those earthly achievements pale out in insignificance, what will be left will be God's word and plan not men's acclaim or reckoning.

What matters will be what will eventually matter!